CHANGE RINGING

Real Change Requires Continuous Learning!

BY

William Bracken, Ph.D.

Printed in Canada.

Canadian Cataloguing in Publication Data

Bracken, William,
  Change ringing

  Includes bibliographical references and index.
  ISBN 1-55212-352-9

  1. Organizational change. I. Title.
HD58.8.B73 2000   658.4'06   C00-910321-X

TRAFFORD

This book was published *on-demand* in cooperation with Trafford Publishing.
On-demand publishing is a unique process and service of making a book available for retail sale to the public taking advantage of on-demand manufacturing and Internet marketing.
On-demand publishing includes promotions, retail sales, manufacturing, order fulfilment, accounting and collecting royalties on behalf of the author.

Suite 6E, 2333 Government St., Victoria, B.C. V8T 4P4, CANADA
Phone   250-383-6864   Toll-free   1-888-232-4444 (Canada & US)
Fax   250-383-6804   E-mail   sales@trafford.com
Web site   www.trafford.com TRAFFORD PUBLISHING IS A DIVISION OF TRAFFORD HOLDINGS LTD.
Trafford Catalogue #00-0016 www.trafford.com/robots/00-0016.html

10   9   8   7   6   5   4   3

ACKNOWLEDGEMENTS

I would like to thank my childhood family — parents Bernard and Genevieve, brother Patrick, sisters Mary and Genny — for helping me become who I am. Additionally, I would like to thank my family, especially my wife Marsha, son George and daughters Kasey and Kerry for their love, encouragement, humor and conversation. Last but not least, I appreciate the help of my assistant, Meena Walambe, for preparing this manuscript.

CONTENTS

PREFACE

As an engineer and a businessman with over 28 years of industry experience, I have been challenged by the need to implement change during the early stages of my career. The implement change challenge was departmental, while the later stages have involved more organizational change. My initial attempts as a Change Leader were not successful. When I considered why was I not successful, I discovered that the more I pressed people, the more objections and resistances were displayed. Therefore, I began reading on implementation and I returned to school to receive more information and professional certifications in business, quality, engineering and business auditing.

During these post-graduate studies, I read books and articles regarding a wide variety of topics. Topics such as management, business, strategy, planning, quality, technology, corporate culture, psychology, ethics, finance, innovation, implementing change, coaching, teambuilding, leadership, communication and coordination. In 1992 I began collecting notes for my Ph.D. book. The subject I had chosen for my book was to be a study of how to produce quality in the automotive supplier industry. My earlier training as a quality engineer and as a reliability engineer suggested that a focus on tools or particular methods was the key ingredient in the recipe for quality. However, as I studied more, I realized that even though the tools and methods for implementing changes to a more quality focused organization with continuous quality improvement of products was implemented, it was not possible to pursue organizational change without a skilled workforce. More importantly, I realized that involving each person as an agent for change should lead to operational success.

The involvement of each individual in the change process required a greater personal understanding of how to implement change, not just the technical tools involved but individually and personally focused. At this point, I concluded that a Change Leader that is required to successfully lead organizational transformation should be skillful in multiple areas in order to deal with multiple people and situations.

This individual preparation by a Change Leader is required because change is an inescapable fact of life that requires each person to develop personal understanding and to pursue continuous preparation. The ability to lead organization changes involves personal preparation to properly change the business and to influence other individuals. This book contains material, previously recorded in the personal diaries of a Change Leader that was used

This material that was collected during a six-year period involves technical, social, philosophical and business disciplines. The material is a mixture of data, observations, literature reviews, case history, and interpretations of the multiple information sources that I used as a Change Leader in developing suitable reactions to a changing business requirement.

INTRODUCTION

Why Another Book Dealing with Change Management

Implementing change is a topic that has received considerable attention in the press during the past few years. My interest in the topic of change was intensified when I was assigned the task of implementing a total business quality system. During each phase of the project, I found that each article or book that I read provided some new information, or at the very least a variation on some previously acquired information that had not been considered.

The project resulted in the successful implementation of a new business quality system that required ongoing maintenance and refinements. Both the implementation and the continuation of the system have required changes in thinking, structure, assignments and workloads. These changes were implemented with great difficulty and have required continuous improvement accompanied by continuous difficulty.

My experience, reading and reflection has taught me that a Change Leader must be prepared to guide organizational change by emphasizing personal growth for himself/herself and other members of the organization. The development of suitable reactions to the changes that influence both business and personal life requires that a leader thoughtfully explore multiple subjects and assimilate the information into a cohesive structure. Both business and personal development are mentioned because implementing change involves people and their capacity for change is influenced by their knowledge in their particular field of business and their personal opinions, beliefs, prejudices and conduct.

I found that personal and business development requires the review and analysis of available literature, particularly in those specific technological areas relevant to your career. However, I also discovered that the success of your career is not based solely on your technological powers, but rather is more dependant on your ability to understand and cope with the change of technology or business process and the influence on those individuals involved.

The problem then is, not how to implement change but, "How do we as individuals understand people, cultures, business, and technology to develop a business structure to prepare for change?" Specifically, significant business operation changes required by new customer standards, requires leadership that is skilled in multiple disciplines. This is particularly true when an individual works in a bi-cultural environment, such as I do. Real change begins with ourselves.

I previously mentioned that I have been involved in implementing change during my career. My recent experience was the most comprehensive because I was required to lead a transformation of an organization. The transformation involved a change from a small organization, organized on an ad-hoc basis, to a structured, continuously improving organization, which is independently certified and is required to maintain certification as judged by independent auditors. I possessed adequate knowledge of the standards, quality tools, statistics and operations to initiate change; but I experienced resistance to change that substantially slowed the transformation.

At first I thought that the resistance to change would simply be corrected by explaining why we needed to change and followed by distribution of information. I mistakenly thought that everyone would recognize the importance and follow my agenda.

Unfortunately, this approach was wrong because I failed to recognize individual agendas, capacity, motivation, background, needs and rewards. I began thinking that the development of individual understanding, capabilities, and attitude are required to maintain focus and to permit the successful improvement of business, career, and personal lives. The improvement can be compromised whenever an individual is not adequately prepared and lacks a road map on how to adjust to changing conditions. This book provides inspirational and varied messages that I found to be helpful, along with some specific guidelines to follow growth in multiple areas.

A case history, involving the transformation of an automotive supplier to a documented business system, is provided as an example of the interrelationship between individual and organizational change.

Project management tools are very useful for tracking and reporting an organizational transformation. However, if the individuals within the organization are not prepared or have different agendas, then project reporting will simply report delay after delay. A broad multi-disciplinary review of topics is very helpful in dealing with obstacles to change because business, career, and personal experiences are interrelated. Knowledge in technical, legal, psychological, cultural, historical, spiritual and philosophical areas must be combined with life experiences and thoughtful contemplation to develop effective responses. This book then is an effort to provide such a collection, which when reviewed and combined with the reader's own thoughtful consideration will provide an improved ability to deal with change.

The book also provides a first-hand account of the difficulties encountered and lessons learned when a bi-cultural international automotive supplier office applies the requirements of a new business process, QS-9000, to its sales/engineering/distribution center.

In a broader frame, I believe that human beings must be adaptable to change, but people resist change because they do not know how to adapt. People recognize physical or biological changes, disease or weather, however, change involving work patterns and reporting relationships are more complex for the individual because the change may involve physical, biological, social, cultural and technological areas. Coping with complex change involving people requires broad based knowledge developed from reading and studying varied information combined with contemplative analysis. The change preparation of the individuals, who are required to participate/nor lead the transformation of an organization, can lead to the success or failure of a company's efforts. Therefore, it is very important for all members of the organization, but especially for transformation leaders, to acquire knowledge combined with contemplative thought so that their capability to implement business and workplace changes can be less stressful and more meaningful.

The organizational change involved business process changes or better definition of individual roles, responsibilities, requirements and reporting. An industry standard called QS-9000 was used as the model to develop the new business operating system. The QS-9000 standard is based on an international standard, ISO-9000, but is more extensive. It was decided that the best way to introduce the QS-9000 based business operating system was to also include aspects of Management By Objectives (MBO) and Total Quality Management. Since these terms, that are commonly used in the automotive industry are not universally familiar, then the following explanations will be helpful.

1.   ISO 9000

A quality management and quality assurance standard developed as an

international document by the "International Organization for Standardization".

ISO 9000, in this book, is also used as a reference term for the ISO 9000 series of

standards. "The ISO 9000 series consists of five documents: three core quality system

documents which are models of quality assurance, namely, ISO 9001/Q91, ISO

9002/Q92, and ISO 9003/Q93 and two supporting guidelines documents, ISO 9000/Q90

and ISO 9004/Q94."[1] The series of standards (9000-9004) are not *technical in content* in

that they do not specify nor set criteria – i.e., minimum purity, pH tolerances, hardness

requirements, etc., for products. Rather, the quality system standard 9001/Q91,

9002/Q92 and 9003/Q93, "complement relevant product or service requirements given in

the technical specifications" (ANSI/ASQC Standard Q90-1987, p.1). Each standard

focuses on the documentation of operational techniques and managerial activities used to

fulfill customer expectations and requirements."[2]

2.   QS-9000

An American automotive industry quality system requirement that uses the ISO

9000 series as a basis. The standard's name, Quality System, suggests that its

applicability is to the quality function or department, when, in fact, the standard involves

a business system. "AETNA discovered ISO 9000 defined a business management

system, not just a quality management system."[3]

---

[1] Lamprecht, James L. *ISO 9000 Preparing for Registration*. Milwaukee: ASQC Quality Press, 1992. P. 3.
[2] Lamprecht, James L. *ISO 9000 Preparing for Registration*. Milwaukee: ASQC Quality Press, 1992. P. 4.
[3] Chowdhury, Subir., and Zimmer, Ken. *QS-9000 Process*. Chicago: Irwin, 1996. P. 53

3.   MBO

MBO is an acronym for "Management By Objectives". MBO is a systems approach to management that involves looking at the entire process. First, objectives are defined which may be social, political, technical, personal, spiritual, financial, economical, or any combination. Second, objectives are measured and third, the system provides feedback for adjustments.

MBO is sometimes considered as simply an individual performance review process of goal setting. The process of goal setting for individuals is one aspect of a business MBO, but the actual meaning is broader involving a business philosophy.

"Management By Objectives isn't an additional company program appended to or layered over the existing structure. It forces a relationship between all units and becomes a way of life. The attempt to treat it as a mechanistic program, encased in a twice-a-year interview bubble, is probably the greatest cause of its misuse and failure. But seen systematically, MBO can change the character and direction of the organization for the better."[4]

4.   TQM

TQM is an acronym for "Total Quality Management". TQM is a "cooperative form of operating an organization in a way that relies on the talents of both labor and management to continually improve quality and productivity using teams and facts in decision making." [5]

[4] Odiorne, George S. *MBO II A System of Managerial Leadership for the 80s.* Belmont: Fearon Pitman, 1979. P. 313.
[5] Schmidt, Warren H., and Finnigan, Jerome P. *TQManager*. San Francisco: Jossey-Bass, 1993. P. 122.

TQM involves the use of multiple practices to achieve the goal of a successful, productive, and confident organization. The theories and practices that influence TQM are as follows:

- "*Scientific management* taught us how to seek the best way to do a job by measuring time, motion, and results.
- *Group dynamics* taught us how to unleash the mental and emotional power of a group to solve problems.
- *Training and development* gave us insights into how people learn and showed us how to design effective learning experiences of adults.
- *Achievement motivation theory* made us aware of how much satisfaction we get from accomplishing something.
- *Employee involvement strategies* helped us to learn that workers become more responsible when they can influence the way their organization works and the way they do their jobs.
- *Linking-pin organizations*, a concept of Rensis Likert (1967), conceived of organizations as a series of overlapping teams in which each manager is a leader of one group and a member of another.
- *Sociotechnical systems* made us think of organizations as systems in which every part is interdependent with every other part.
- *Organization development* theory and practice taught us how to think about change and how to help a whole organization identify and diagnose its problems and learn to improve.
- *Corporate culture* literature made us aware of the power of beliefs and myths influencing people to decide on their priorities and do their work.
- *New leadership theory* taught us the difference between leading and managing – and the importance of vision, trust, and empowerment in mobilizing human effort.
- *Strategic planning* gave us the technology to map an organization's environment and to plan its development in a systematic way."[6]

---

[6] Schmidt, Warren H., and Finnigan, Jerome P. *TQManager*. San Francisco: Jossey-Bass, 1993. P. 24.

Chapter 1

What is Change Ringing and a Change Leader

The dictionary defines the term "Change Ringing" as the ringing of a chime of bells to a set series of different combinations so that no one sequence is rung twice. Therefore, the title "Change Ringing" was selected to represent the multiple conditions that influence the capability of a Change Leader to effect an organizational transformation. The changing conditions apply to business operations, people interactions, customer requirements, market, technological conditions, personal health and welfare. All of these factors influence a person's adaptability and balance.

An individual's attitude and capability adjusts with new personal and workplace experiences and acquired knowledge. The individual who is responsible for leading change or transforming an organization to new business process is assigned a goal to achieve. However, the satisfaction of the goal involving new business process requires systematic thinking because many individuals and departments are involved. "Systematic thinking recognizes that there are many phenomena in life and knowledge, but it starts from a new assumption: It recognizes all phenomena are related to one another and all are part of a whole. A mechanistic approach on the other hand, treats such things as being unrelated and encased in bubbles."[7] Since systematic thinking requires an examination of the whole, then it follows that the examination of a leader responsible for change must involve an exploration of the whole person and process.

---

[7] Odiorne, George S. *MBO II A System of Managerial Leadership for the 80s.* Belmont: Fearon Pitman, 1979. P. 304.

This approach is intuitively correct and as Eric Hoffer said, "To become different from what we are, we must have some awareness of what we are."[8] Therefore, the leader's background is a contributing influence to the ability to affect change because we are considering the whole person. Both current and previous situations influence a Change Leader. The following passage provides some interesting information that the leader must keep pace with recent events.

"The leadership style of a management is often as much a function of a situational background as it is of individual manager's initiative or taste. Managers influence the environment and are in-turn influenced by it. Very often they are still responding to the culture of the past decade when the new one lands upon them, in part because problems and solutions require some lead-time and such time appears to be collapsing on management. The management of the fifties seemed to be responding to the militant labor climate of the thirties, while the labor-market climate was filled with concerns of managing engineers and scientists. The management of the sixties responded well to the needs of the fifties in managing high-talent employees such as engineers and scientists, while outside their offices a racial revolution was going on. In the seventies, management was responding admirably to the racial pressures of the sixties at a time when the feminist pressures of the seventies were ringing about them. The management of the seventies was also busily responding to the counterculture of the sixties, wearing long side-burns and more casual clothes, as the generation of the seventies – more square and work oriented than ever before – came along out of college."[9] Therefore, an

---

[8] Braude, Jacob M. *Complete Speaker's and Toastmaster's Library.*
Paramus, N.J.: Prentice Hall, 1992. P. 94. Volume 3.
[9] Odiorne, George S. *MBO II A System of Managerial Leadership for the 80s.*
Belmont: Fearon Pitman, 1979. P. 20.

exploration of the whole person is necessary to understand how a Change Leader develops.

Based on this information, then it is necessary for me to explain my background in order for you to understand me as a Change Leader. A review of my background will allow you to contrast and compare your own experiences. This process will be useful as you subsequently review the inspirational messages and consider their relevance.

My first such influence on my career and personal adult life was from my parents, who emphasized attending college and earning a degree. My father used to say,

"Bill, study hard, attend school, graduate with a degree in engineering and this will allow you to have a better life than me!"

This statement made sense to me, particularly, since I was raised in the lower-middle class where an emphasis was placed on obtaining a good job.

My parents decided that preparing for college required attending a Catholic elementary school where the no-nonsense approach of nuns would provide the proper educational and spiritual focus for even the most undisciplined mind. Eight years of parochial school attendance during the late 50's and early 60's produced just such a focus. The demanding educational training was indeed an excellent preparation for high school and college. On the other hand, the spiritual teaching was a mixed blessing for me. The discussions about salvation involving a loving and forgiving God were very comforting and appealing. However, the spiritual curriculum at that time placed a strong emphasis on certain damnation that was associated with various conducts. Certain damnation was certainly not a blessing and, in fact, contributed to my feelings of guilt and unworthiness. Today, the Catholic church does not over emphasize the going to hell mentality, which is a big change compared to the teachings of the 1950's and 1960's. The children attending parochial school today are perhaps not as likely to view their religious education as a mixed blessing, as I did.

In 1965 I finished the eighth grade at St. Valentines' school, where I was an honor-roll student. I then entered a public school. Public schools, as I had been led to believe, were filled with undisciplined and uncaring individuals who were unconcerned with either future careers or spiritual grace. This new school, exposure to new attitudes, new feelings about girls, the changing nature of society during the late 60's and my previous developed feelings of guilt and unworthiness all contributed to increase my inner turmoil and force me to consider the changing nature of myself and others.

During the 1960's, society had begun to change, as Figures 1, 2, and 3 indicate. Families were breaking up with a correspondent negative economic impact on families. Additionally, recreational sex seemed to be increasing, as evidenced by the out-of-wedlock birth rate. These social changes were in violation of the rules that I was taught in my religious education. My initial response to these social changes was to be unsympathetic, to those affected due to a belief that simply following the rules that I learned would allow correction. As time went on and I acquired more knowledge, I realized that simply following the rules was not the answer to a situation that probably had several contributing factors such as the encouragement provided by per child welfare payment increases and changes in society's emphasis on forced marriage. I am not going to attempt to explain the exact cause for such social change, but simply indicate its presence and influence on me. Other terms, which were indicators of social change at

Figure 1 – U.S. Divorce Rate[10]

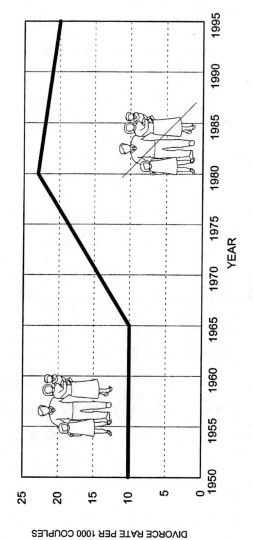

U.S. DIVORCE RATE

Note: One million children experience divorce or seperation each year in the 1990's.

[10] Whitehead, Barbara D. "Dan Quayle Was Right" *Atlantic Magazine*, April 1993, P. 50

Figure 2 –Economic Effect of Divorce[11]

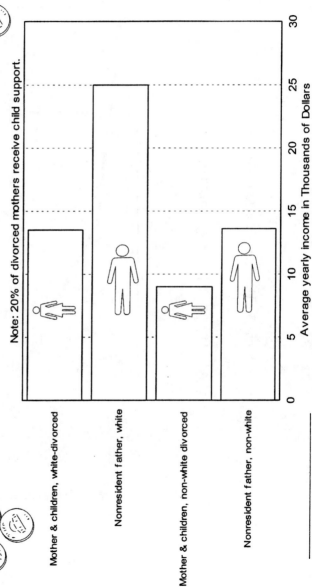

ECONOMIC EFFECT OF DIVORCE

Note: 20% of divorced mothers receive child support.

Mother & children, white-divorced

Nonresident father, white

Mother & children, non-white divorced

Nonresident father, non-white

Average yearly income in Thousands of Dollars

0   5   10   15   20   25   30

[11] Whitehead, Barbara D. "Dan Quayle Was Right" *Atlantic Magazine*, April 1993, P. 50

Figure 3 – U.S. Out of Wedlock Births[12]

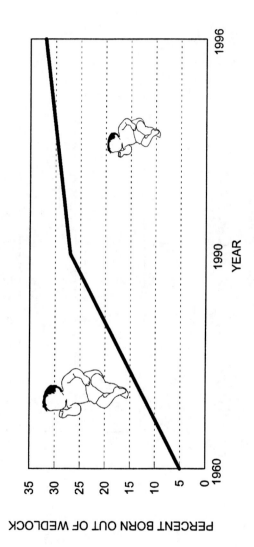

U.S. OUT OF WEDLOCK BIRTHS

[12] Whitehead, Barbara D. "Dan Quayle Was Right" *Atlantic Magazine*, April 1993, P. 50
Unknown. "Families Without Kids", The Economist, November 27, 1999. P. 27.

that time were welfare, drugs, Vietnam, hippies, groupies, riots, and peaceful demonstrations. The ideas represented by these terms challenged my viewpoints and my understanding of the world and my place in it. For me, coping with this situation required the avoidance of certain philosophies and individuals that did not fit my background and in-progress maturation. I chose to focus my attention in areas, which were more comfortable and less threatening; but which still permitted a limited expanding awareness, although I sometimes felt guilty about my avoidance approach.

I began attending a Detroit area four-year commuter college in the fall of 1969 with the conviction to become a mechanical engineer. This choice of profession has served me well over the years; however, I do consider the career choice to be biased and substantially influenced by the opinions of my father and older brother. Actually, I was much more interested in history and geography during my elementary and high school years, and possibly would have chosen a college curriculum that involved those subjects. However, I chose engineering because of the excellent job potential and I was strong in science and math. I cannot blame my father or my brother for the choice, since the educational choice was mine. The decision to choose engineering was just easier; I accepted their opinions and followed their advice.

I received three job offers when I graduated from college in 1973 with a degree in mechanical engineering. Chrysler, Ford, and Firestone offered me positions in their Engineering Departments. The Firestone position was in Plant Engineering, while Chrysler and Ford were in Product Engineering. At that time, the Product Engineering positions were considered more challenging, rewarding, and of higher-esteem value than Plant Engineering positions. Because of these considerations, the choice of company was easily narrowed to one of the two car companies. The selection between Chrysler and Ford was simplified by two facts.

1.   Ford paid 20% more money
2.   Ford was closer to my home and in a much more desirable neighborhood

These considerations resulted in a selection of Ford Motor Company as my employer. Here again the pragmatic reasoning, be smart decision process, which have been emphasized by the schools and my parents was utilized. The dream, emotional and gut level feeling that favored Chrysler was suppressed. I accepted the smart choice of Ford and I overlooked my dream, as I had my earlier dreams of studying history and geography. Economically, the choice of an engineer was proven to be the smart choice, as my father had said. (See Figure 4)

My chosen employer, Ford Motor Company – Transmission Division, was and is an excellent engineering environment. Good design and development engineers coupled with knowledgeable technicians, dedicated mechanics, talented designers, and excellent test facilities provided me with a very practical, no nonsense, and blue-collar atmosphere. I learned the value of hard work, dedication, and of self-sacrifice. The self-sacrifice aspect involved heavy overtime, which was similar to my college years of long hours of working, attending school, and completing homework. I began my career under the mistaken impression that having graduated from a locally prestigious university with strong affiliations to the automotive industry would entitle me to work forty hours per week and enjoy life. This belief was gradually eroded by the nearly constant fifty-eight hour workweek, and my nagging doubt that the job was never finished. My belief in reasonable work hours was influenced by the knowledge that the general trend in the

Figure 4 – U. S. Salary Survey[13]

U.S. SALARY SURVEY
INFORMATION FROM U.S. NEWS & WORLD REPORT 11/1/93

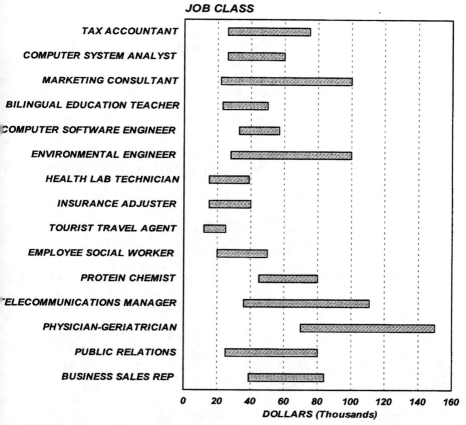

NOTE: Physician salaries can reach $250,000
depending on location of practice and total training.

[13] Beddingfield, Katherine T., Hawkins Dana, Watson, Andrea R., "Hot Tracks In 20 Professions"
U.S. News and World Report, November 1, 1993. P. 106

world was reduced hours, as Figure 5 indicates. It is noticeable, however, that the hours in the United States are not substantially different over a thirty (30) year period. The long grinding hours and the doubt sapped my energy and caused depression, insomnia, irritability, withdrawal from personal contacts, and eventually a divorce from a short three year marriage to my high school sweetheart.

The divorce was particularly traumatic for me because of the following:

1. The first in my family (of one brother and two sisters) to be divorced
2. Catholic teaching had preached firmly against divorce
3. I married my high school sweetheart
4. Job stress, particularly, since this was my first engineering job
5. Lack of leisure time since I had bought a house and all the maintenance that goes with it.

Due to these reasons, the divorce was very painful and caused me to question myself even more than I had done in the past. Ever since parochial elementary school, I had developed an increasing habit of questioning my actions, beliefs, and capabilities. It was at this time that I began searching for knowledge to cope and direct. Oftentimes I felt threatened in my career and only recently discovered that this is a common concern. I began reading articles and books concerning a variety of topics so that I could better understand myself and others, to improve my chances of success, and to permit me a more enjoyable life. While I did not possess a clear picture of how the knowledge puzzle fit together, I did have a sense of the importance of gaining knowledge and subsequently improving my chances of emotional and financial success. My intuition regarding the need to consider how I could improve my financial position was eventually proven by a variety of economic data. The data provided in Figure 6 indicates that the price of a major

19

Figure 5 – Annual Hours Worked in Manufacturing[14]

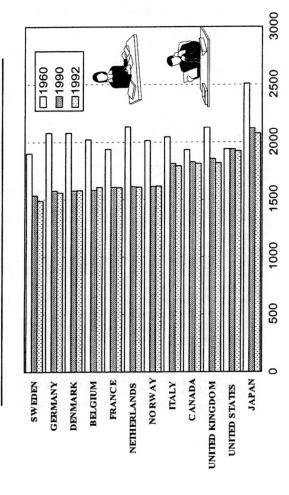

ANNUAL HOURS WORKED IN MANUFACTURING

[14] Sorge Marjorie. "UAW Walks A Tightrope Between Old And New Jobs." *Wards Auto World,* June 1993. P. 38

consumer product, automobiles, continues advancing relative to family income. The data

shows that the average price of a new car dropped relative to income in the 1970's and

1980's, before starting to climb again. Therefore, advancing your income becomes

critical just to maintain a standard of living. However, I decided that knowledge was the

goal and that money would likely follow. I sought knowledge in mathematics, statistics,

engineering materials, product design, business operations, organizational design,

psychology, philosophy, communications, medicine, and quality. Along the way, I

acquired the following credentials to accompany my bachelor degree in engineering.

- Master's Degree in Administration
- Registered Professional Engineer
- Certified Reliability Engineer
- Certified Quality Engineer
- Certified Quality Auditor
- Doctor of Philosophy in Business Administration

I should mention that these professional accomplishments occurred even while I remarried and I was:

1. Raising 3 children
2. Being directly involved in years (10) of coping with a serious life threatening condition that affected my wife
3. Working 50-70 hours per week
4. Changing jobs twice
5. Coping with parental illness
6. Working in a highly stressed work environment due to a corporate buyout

The professional accomplishments are a recognized acknowledgment, but actually were not the most helpful. The most helpful activity for me was when I began to record in my diaries the life thoughts, organizational advice, business comments and educational comments that I have found during my years of studying and reading. Herein I offer my record that I have accumulated and continue to accumulate in my lifelong learning that has helped adjust to "Change Ringing". The material is generally written as separate records, which do not flow as in a novel but must be read and thoughtfully considered. The sequence of the material has been established to encourage this consideration. This material involves a single thought compilation constructed from consideration of multiple readings. In other cases, I have provided specific credit. In all cases, I have tried to be accurate and to give proper acknowledgment in the footnotes or in the works cited. As my life has changed in a random fashion just as the church bells do, as defined by "Change Ringing", I have found this type of inspirational material to be a valuable guide. I offer this material not as a person's only guide, but simply helpful messages to understand and cope with life's change ringing. The value of the material was expressly apparent when the implementation of an organizational change to a new business system required a Change Leader.

Figure 6 – United States Median Family Income and New Car Price[15]

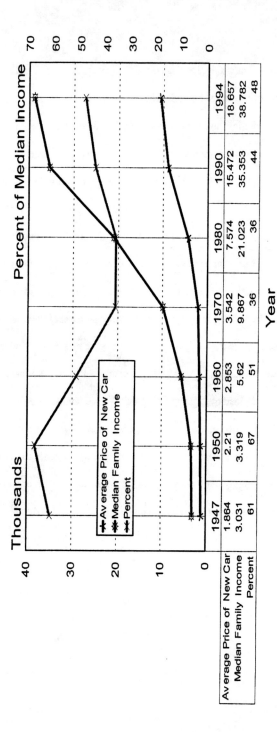

United States Median Family Income and New Car Price

	1947	1950	1960	1970	1980	1990	1994
Average Price of New Car	1.864	2.21	2.853	3.542	7.574	15.472	18.657
Median Family Income	3.031	3.319	5.62	9.867	21.023	35.353	38.782
Percent	61	67	51	36	36	44	48

Thousands

Percent of Median Income

Year

Average Price of New Car
Median Family Income
Percent

[15] Lienert, Paul. "Family Income Needed to Buy Cars Is Rising Again." *Detroit News*, August 21, 1996.

Chapter 2

The Change Leader and Change Management

The topic of dealing with change is a very broad subject involving many

interrelated dimensions such as the following:

- Social
- Cultural
- Financial
- Organizational
- Psychological
- Technological
- Biological
- Economical
- Spiritual
- Legal
- Physical

Such a broad subject area seems to be less capable of study by hard quantitative

analytical principles and more amenable to study using the case study approach. I

believe that significant organizational change requires a single committed Change Leader

who is capable of integrating and applying the multiple dimensions to improve the

operations of the bi-cultural sales / engineering / distribution office of an international

company.

My particular situation as described above, may be different than yours; however,

I believe that my message is applicable to many individuals. Sometimes a book such as

this is thought of as a case study approach, which involves the analysis of the reactions of

specific individuals or companies experiencing significant change. Case studies may be

limited because the particular study covers a specific time period. As an example, the

1984 book "In Search of Excellence" written by T. Peters and R. Waterman, studied companies that were considered excellent masters of accommodating change and growing the business. Now, in 2000, some of those excellent companies are not considered excellent. What happened? How do companies adequately prepare for change given the complex web of change dimensions? The simple answer is that companies do not prepare for change, people do. Excellent companies require, at least, some excellent people and excellent systems. Therefore, the multidimensional continuing education and refinement of individuals, which will permit greater understanding and development of change coping strategies is the necessary ingredient to continued corporate success. Individual ability leads to corporate ability providing adequate consideration is given to teamwork.

The inspirational material that follows is a collection of information taken from the works cited, the general sources of information listed below, and combined with my personal experience. The general sources of information listed below were reviewed on a regular basis and contributed many thought-provoking ideas. It is not possible to specifically list all articles that have been digested, particularly, in the past six years. Therefore, suffice to say that multiple general sources of information were used on a regular basis to increase personal awareness, understanding, and refinement of change coping strategies.

The general sources that were used and continue to be used are as follows:

- Business Week Magazine
- Time
- U.S. News and World Report
- Detroit Free Press (newspaper)
- Industry Week Magazine –
- Quality Progress Magazine
- Machine Design Magazine
- Training Magazine
- Fortune Magazine
- The Economist Magazine
- Circuit Assembly Magazine
- Nikkei Weekly (Japanese newspaper)
- Strategy and Business
- Ward's Auto World Magazine
- Automotive Industries Magazine
- Design News Magazine
- Harvard Business Review Magazine
- Electronic Business Magazine
- Automotive News
- Far Eastern Economic Review Magazine
- Quality Digest Magazine
- Economist
- Journal of Innovative Management

The Works Cited List provides specific material that was found to be useful in the implementation of changes that were required to accomplish the transformation of an automotive supplier organization. The specific change that required leadership concerned the implementation of an automotive business standard, QS-9000, to an organization that was unfamiliar and unconvinced of the need. The QS-9000 business process system involved the implementation of a more comprehensive business system suitable for a medium sized business. This system was quite a change from the previous system that can best be described as a loosely organized small business relying on an individual talent with loose accountability. As has been implied, this system change was dynamic and involved many factors including the Change Leader's experience, interests, and capabilities.

As I briefly explained in the introduction, I decided that the implementation of a business operating system would be based on the customer required QS-9000 standard, but would also include consideration of other items, ISO-9000, TQM and MBO. The introduction only provided a brief definition of the other items. This brief definition does not provide sufficiently detailed descriptions to provide you with the quality background knowledge needed to understand the nature of the business and individual changes required. Therefore, I will now provide a more detailed description of quality standards and principles that could actually be better described as business operating system descriptions.

The American automotive industry require that their suppliers be certified to the QS-9000 Quality System Standard. The QS-9000 standard is based on ISO 9000 and includes elements, which are similar to the American Baldrige Quality Award. While QS-9000, ISO 9000, and the Baldrige Award criteria are each identified somehow with "Quality Systems", they contain the format for a good business operating system.

The first edition of the QS-9000 system standard was published in 1994 and the third edition was recently published in 1998.

In September 1994, Chrysler, Ford, and General Motors unveiled QS-9000. This new quality system model places great emphasis on customer satisfaction and will affect companies that manufacture or supply components and other products for the Big Three.

Under the guidelines of QS-9000, suppliers must change their quality systems to meet the automakers' expectations. QS-9000 is a blend of Chrysler's Supplier Quality

Assurance Manual, Ford's Q-101 Quality System Standard, and General Motors' North American Operations' Targets for Excellence. The heart of the new quality system model centers upon ISO 9000, the international quality standard.

"The arrival of QS-9000 has set the stage for change throughout the auto industry. The effects of the new quality system requirements will be felt by thousands of auto suppliers in the United States, Canada, and Mexico. Eventually, registration to QS-9000 and ISO 9000 will be mandated – General Motors has already set a December 1997 deadline."

"Suppliers are required to implement the Ford QOS methodology. QOS is a systematic approach that uses standardized tools and practices to manage the business and ultimately, improve customer satisfaction."[16]

The specific benefits obtainable with implementation of ISO 9000 and by relationship extension, QS-9000 was identified by the automotive supplier as follows:

a) Reduce waste and provide for quality improvement using customer focus in a total business framework. An office/facility cannot be excellent in the sense of having arrived at permanent excellence, it is always in a state of practicing the discipline of learning, a discipline of ISO 9000 guidelines will assist in providing this focus.

b) Provide a focus for involvement and improvement by all personnel that can lead to greater flexibility and provide a feeling of personal accomplishments.

---

[16] Unknown. *QS-9000*. Automotive Engineering: Warrendale, PA. SAE: June 1995. P. 61-65.

c) Improve traceability of products, drawings, and contracts and significant issues.

d) Promote consistency of business discipline at local facilities that will assist location-to-location communication.

e) Gain customer and employee admiration by the ability to demonstrate business intelligence.

f) Providing an organized system that will lead to increased efficiency and the ability to transfer people and programs with minimal disruption to operations.

The particular areas of importance identified by ISO 9000 that forms the basis of QS-9000 are as follows:

4.1   Management Responsibility

4.2   Quality System

4.3   Contract Review

4.4   Design Control

4.5   Document and Data Control

4.6   Purchasing

4.7   Control of Customer Supplied Product

4.8   Product Identification and Traceability

4.9   Process Control

4.10   Inspection and Testing

4.11   Control of Inspection, Measuring and Test Equipment

4.12   Inspection and Test Status

4.13   Control of Nonconforming Product

4.14   Corrective and Preventive Action

4.15   Handling, Storage, Packaging, Preservation and Delivery

4.16   Control of Quality Records

4.17   Internal Quality Audits

4.18   Training

4.19   Servicing

4.20   Statistical Techniques

A review of these sections reveals that the ISO 9000 and QS-9000 standards extend beyond the quality function and include Engineering, Sales, Distribution, Human Resources, Service, Purchasing, and Management. The standard describes a business operating system based on quality principles.

The Baldrige Quality System also contains numerous categories that are assessed at each company that applies for the award. The QS-9000 standard does not make any reference to Baldrige, however, since the Baldrige Award approach was being considered by the automotive supplier as a potential tool to use for organizational transformation, then it was necessary to review Baldrige categories, which are as follows:

Categories[17]

1.0   Leadership

1.1   Senior Executive Leadership

1.2   Management for Quality

1.3   Public Responsibility

---

[17] George, Stephen. The Baldrige Quality System. New York: John Wiley & Sons, 1997. P. 44

2.0   **Information and Analysis**

     2.1   Scope and Management of Quality and Performance Data and Information

     2.2   Competitive Comparisons and Benchmarks

     2.3   Analysis of Uses of Company-Level Data

3.0   **Strategic Quality Planning**

     3.1   Strategic Quality and Company Performance Planning Process

     3.2   Quality and Performance Plans

4.0   **Human Resource Development and Management**

     4.1   Human Resource Management

     4.2   Employee Involvement

     4.3   Employee Education and Training

     4.4   Employee Performance and Recognition

     4.5   Employee Well-Being and Morale

5.0   **Management of Process Quality**

     5.1   Design and Introduction of Quality products and Services

     5.2   Process Management - Product and Service Production and Delivery Processes

     5.3   Process Management – Business Processes and Support Services

     5.4   Supplier Quality

     5.5   Quality Assessment

6.0   **Quality and Operational Results**

    6.1   Product and Service Quality Results

    6.2   Company Operational Results

    6.3   Business Process and Support Service Results

    6.4   Supplier Quality Results

7.0   **Customer Focus and Satisfaction**

    7.1   Customer Relationship Management

    7.2   Commitment to Customers

    7.3   Customer Satisfaction Determination

    7.4   Customer Satisfaction Results

    7.5   Customer Satisfaction Comparisons

    7.6   Future Requirements and Expectations of Customers

The benefits of the Baldrige Award have been debated and suffice it to say that there is disagreement regarding benefits. Mr. George states the following in his book:

> "No group has been more frustrated with senior management than quality professionals, who have long struggled to find effective strategies for involving management in quality. John Cooney, manager of the Xerox's National Quality Communications and Promotions Office, has been sharing the Xerox story with companies since Xerox won the Baldrige Award in 1989. He has heard the plea."

"The most frequent concern expressed by companies we talk to is leadership," says Cooney. "If the leader's fingerprints aren't on the quality strategy, the propensity for failure is great."

Quality systems fail because of management's apathy and ignorance. For a long time, management could afford to be apathetic about quality because profitability could be bought by sheer volume and besides, it had a quality department in charge of that quality stuff. As a result, management ignored quality with obvious consequences: ignoring leads to ignorance.

The first category of the Baldrige criteria does not reward apathy or ignorance. On the contrary, it recognizes leadership as the driver of a company's quality system. If your company's leaders are merely passengers, no one will drive you anywhere, and total quality management will not even be on your map. But if your leaders believe, as others do, that quality products and services are your ticket into the competition, they have their work cut out for them. They must lead the change."[18]

The Baldrige criteria emphasizes leadership and the QS-9000 standard indicates that management responsibility is the first criteria to be considered. Therefore, there is agreement in the fundamental principle of the primary importance of leadership. However, there are many theories of leadership such as Theory X, Theory Y, Path-Goal Theory, and situational leadership. The specific differences in these theories are not the issue. The issue is, "What disciplined approach is required by the Change Leader so that

---

[18] George, Stephen. The Baldrige Quality System. New York: John Wiley & Sons, 1997. P. 57-58

a significant change to a business operating system can be affected?" The answer is

contained in the following quotes:

> "In managing, as in any other field, unless practitioners are to learn
> only through trial and error, there is no other place they can turn to for
> meaningful guidance than the accumulated knowledge underlying their
> practice. Yet, in managing, much confusion remains about the nature of
> managerial knowledge. Questions are often raised about whether
> management is a science or an art, what theory exists, and in what way it
> can be useful to managers, how technology fits into theory and science,
> and why there are so many schools or approaches to management theory
> and knowledge. What can managers believe, and how can this belief be
> useful to them?

> **Both Art and Science.** While these questions are often raised, a
> moment of reflection will indicate that they are really rather meaningless.
> Managing like all other practices, is an art. It is know-how. It is doing
> things in the light of the realities of a situation. But the practice of
> managing must make use of underlying organized knowledge; and it is
> this knowledge, whether crude or advanced, whether exact or inexact,
> which, to the extent that it is well-organized; clear, and pertinent,
> constitutes a science. Thus, managing as a practice is art; the organized
> knowledge underlying it may be referred to as science. Consequently,
> science and art are not mutually exclusive; they are complementary."[19]

"As today's corporation evolves, it will need 'renaissance managers' – people

whose vision encompasses, all the activities of the global enterprise." George Fisher,

Motorola's president and CEO, described the "manufacturing renaissance" in a speech at

the Stanford Manufacturing Conference in April 1988. "If you are to be a successful

(renaissance manager), you will demonstrate creativity and technological flair and a deep

understanding of the world's markets and political and economic forces. You will weld

together a team that solves very specific customer needs. You will be a knowledge

engineer, able to grasp a problem and know what technologies are most appropriate for a

specific application. You will demonstrate an ability to envision your strategic intent and

---

[19] Bittle, Lester R., and Ramsey, Jackson E. *Handbook for Professional Managers.*
New York: McGraw-Hill, 1985. P. 507.

energize your organization. You will create an environment that enables your team to succeed. You will attract the best and brightest people to this environment. You will exert a positive influence beyond your company, in your community and in your profession. Above all, you will let your imagination transcend conventional boundaries. That is an intimidating list of qualifications."[20]

Another practice that was reviewed was TQM.

TQM is an acronym for "Total Quality Management". TQM is not a requirement of QS-9000. However, numerous references to TQM were found during the research into the background and development of QS-9000. The definition of terms provided in the introduction provides a brief description of TQM. The definition includes a description of the many influencing theories and practices, which is similar to QS-9000, in which TQM advocates a complete business operating system. The exact content of the system is not specified by TQM, but the need for thorough consideration of multiple disciplines is specified.

"Total Quality Management (TQM) provides a paradigm shift in management philosophy for improving organizational effectiveness (Byrne, 1992; Gagne, 1983; Lowe and Masseo, 1986). TQM focuses the efforts of all members of the organization to continuously improve all organizational processes and increase value to customers, while relying upon a clear vision of the organization's purpose. This depends on the removal of barriers, both within the organization and between the organization and its various

---

[20] George, Stephen. *The Baldrige Quality System*. New York: John Wiley & Sons, 1997. P. 58.

stakeholders. TQM has been embraced by thousands of organizations (Lawler and

Mohrmon, 1992) as an important, new approach to management."[21]

The successful implementation of TQM is influenced by a recognition and

receptiveness to ongoing training and development and the prior state of preparation

(Emery 1996). The specific training and development is an interactive process requiring

an interested management and a receptive employee. This is significant because multi

disciplinary preparation is again recognized as a significant factor in the success of an

organizational transformation.

"Indications are that training is critical for the implementation and successful

sustainment of any new strategy, including TQM. TQM requires a well-educated

workforce and although companies invest heavily in quality awareness and statistical

process control, often the training is too narrowly focused."[22]

Another section in the Ms. Vass article states,

"To successfully implement and sustain TQM, a company must
handle major shifts in culture ..... when implementing TQM, management
can often overlook the importance of employees. A failure to consider
issues at the individual level can ensure failure at the corporate level."[23]

The article by Mr. Vass contains an interesting adaptation of the personal

needs hierarchy postulated by Abraham Maslow in the 1943 article, "A Theory of Human

Motivation". Mr. Maslow's needs hierarchy was prepared as an explanation of human

motivation. The theory is that people are motivated to satisfy needs and that these needs

---

[21] Emery, Charles R.; Summers, Timothy P.; Surak, John G.; *The role of organizational climate in the Implementation of Total Quality Management....*, Vol. 8, Journal of Managerial Issues, 12-22-1996, pp 484(13)
[22] Vass, Dianna J., and Kincade, Doris H. *Relationship of TQM Implementation and Employee Opinion Survey: A Study of Three Manufacturers.* Quality Management Journal: Volume 6, Issue 1, 1999. P. 61.
[23] Vass, Dianna J., and Kincade, Doris H. *Relationship of TQM Implementation and Employee Opinion Survey: A Study of Three Manufacturers.* Quality Management Journal: Volume 6, Issue 1, 1999. P. 62.

exist at different satisfaction levels. The first level is basic needs such as food and shelter, the second level is safety needs such as to remain employed, the third level is social needs which is to be accepted, the forth level is self-fulfillment needs which is self-expression. Peter Drucker's [24] analysis of Maslow's needs contained important insights because Drucker believed that people do work to satisfy needs and that as the needs at the first level are reasonably satisfied, then the person's motivation is likely to be more focused on the next higher levels. However, Drucker added a new belief that was that the person at the second level does not now ignore the first level needs as being totally satisfied because the needs are only reasonably satisfied at this point in time. The continued satisfaction of the first level needs is still important.

Mr. Vass's article takes the Maslow hierarchy of needs for personal motivation and builds a hierarchy of needs for organizational development. A review of the hierarchy, which follows, indicates the importance of learning and attitude to the development of the organization.

---

[24] Drucker, Peter. *Management*. New York: Harper and Row, 1973. P. 195.

Employee needs hierarchy (Adopted from Bennis 1997 and Kottler 1996).[25]

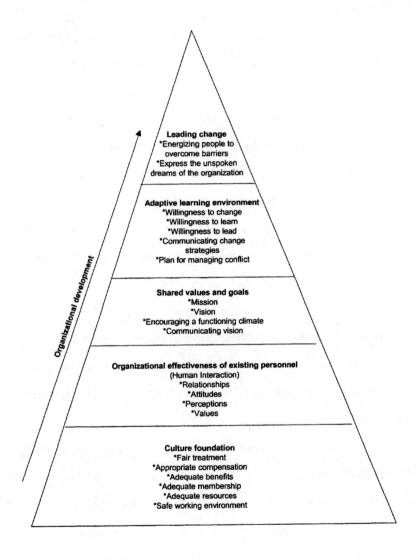

MBO is another technique that was reviewed for influence on the organizational change.

MBO is an acronym for "Management By Objectives". MBO is not a specific requirement of QS-9000, however, the standard does indicate the need for objectives and comparison measurements on the status of goal satisfaction. Therefore, it was hypothesized, that understanding of the essence of MBO may provide guidance useful in the implementation of the QS-9000 organizational transformation.

MBO is a term that, in recent years, has fallen into disuse. Such a simple concept of specifying objectives, measuring status, and providing feedback would seem to be vary appealing to Change Leaders and their organizations. However, when MBO was implemented, the implementation was narrowly defined in scope to deal with employee performance reviews, and not organizational performance.[26]

MBO properly defined then deals with organizational performance, or lack of, and seeks to establish means to effect change by institution objectives and measures. Again, the question of what is involved to effect change was investigated and again the answer was effective management or Change Leader. The definition for this effective Change Leader is as follows:

"One of the most obvious facts about management is that there are effective bosses and ineffective ones. An organization may have an impressive array of experts in engineering, investment, purchasing, accounting, finance, sales, and heaven knows what else, and yet still fall dismally short of its objectives. Yet later, the same organization headed by a different manager (or the same manager using different management

---

[26] Odiorne, George S. *MBO II A System of Managerial Leadership for the 80s.*
Belmont: Fearon Pitman, 1979. P. 316.

methods) will succeed brilliantly. How to achieve this turning around of an organization is thus the subject of much discussion.

One conclusion that has been reached on this question is that *managing* is a function or activity that affects total organizational performance far more than any other. In fact, it makes the functions and activities effective or ineffective.

Another conclusion is that this managerial function is a set of actions and a kind of behavior that is *distinct from the activities it manages.*

How does one learn how to manage? By and large, there are three basic sources of management knowledge: imitation, situational thinking, and behavioral science."[27]

---

[27] Odiorne, George S. *MBO II A System of Managerial Leadership for the 80s* Belmont: Fearon Pitman, 1979. P. 54-55.

Chapter 3

Personal Reflections: An Opinion Developed After Consideration

This chapter is a collection of materials dealing with psychology, personal attitude, socialization, motivation and life balance.

Remember that my premise is that change is constant; therefore, a Change Leader's approach to dealing with change must involve constant and never ending preparation. However, a good understanding of yourself and others is required that provides a base for the ongoing building of a structure to implement change. The ongoing building is achieved by continuous learning accompanied by thoughtful reflection and adjustments to the combinations we all face.

I found that the following material was helpful in refining my foundation, and I hope that you will benefit as well.

Motivational speaker Patrick O'Dooley provided the top ten winning qualities that an individual requires, in order of occurrence:
- Positive attitude
- Enthusiasm
- Determination
- Motivation
- Confidence
- Optimism
- Dedication
- Happiness
- Good listener
- Patience

Look for opportunities in every risk.

There is a continuum of fear provoking behavior that some people use to control others:

- Silence
- Staring
- Ignoring people
- Insulting and putdowns
- Blaming or comments discrediting others
- Aggressiveness not assertiveness
- Threatening

The difficulty of getting heard can be experienced by individuals who are not as persistent as others. These individuals do not speak as forcefully at meetings, or do not begin with a high level of credibility, as a result of their rank, regional or ethnic style differences.

"This life is a test; it is only a test." If it were a real life, you would receive instructions on where to go and what to do. ("source unknown")

Self-discipline and attitude are of prime importance to each individual's career and life success.

People tend to express conclusions without sharing background information. This is a form of arrogance that irritates many people. I call this the know-it-all syndrome.

A disability requires the presence of a physical or mental impairment that substantially affects a major life activity. It is important to remember this when dealing with some employees.

Managing change requires that issues be categorized. One possible way to categorize is as follows:

- Employee centered issues
- Customer centered issues
- Profit issues
- Social issues

"A great artist can paint a great picture on a small canvas." (Charles Warner)

"Men acquire a particular quality by constantly acting in a particular way." (Aristotle)

Lone ranger or lone wolf behavior impedes cooperation. This behavior is more typical of an industrial sales person. Therefore, find ways to foster group cooperation so that the lone wolf is more involved.

Any bit of knowledge may be useful when least expected. This is my theory of problem solving, but this principle has been formalized in the Russian problem solving approach called Triz.

Sharing information allows integration of people. However, sharing information requires communication, which requires establishing common baseline understanding among the communicants first.

Does the teaching of religious values help to prevent social problems? I believe the answer is "yes" because business and personal ethics are intertwined.

Be a take-charge persona with persistence and determination.

Factors affecting morale (Maslow Hierarchy) from lowest to highest needs areas follows:
- Physiological needs (hunger, thirst)
- Safety needs
- Belonging/love needs
- Esteem needs (prestige, success)
- Self-actualization (self-fulfilled)

I believe that Americans work for leisure or personal enjoyment time, which is influenced by self-fulfillment and money.

Each person should control his/her attitude. Life is about how I react to it.

You make the choice to be optimistic or pessimistic.

It is OK to disagree with someone as long as you are not disagreeable.

Always work toward developing helpful relationships instead of destructive relationships.

Uniforms or business dress provide a professional atmosphere by identifying the person as a professional. This identification will help to gain respect from others.

It is very common to care deeply for someone but still not be in a position to give him or her all that they want.

Anger, frustration or resentment hurt your chances for success.

You must change and adapt to new situations.

A simple question for each person to consider is, "What example do you set for others to follow or admire?"

Questions to consider asking others when you are involved in problem or conflict resolution are as follows:

- What is your advice?
- How does the situation look to you?
- What do you think I am overlooking? How can I help?
- What are we hoping to get out of this meeting?
- How would you like me to respond to that?
- What evidence would convince you that is not true?
- Why do you believe my idea won't work?
- Where do we go from here?

Read to renew your mind, exercise to renew your enthusiasm and passion, grow professionally and personally to renew your thinking.

Anger is often prompted by feeling hurt. Feeling hurt may be a function of a misunderstanding. Therefore, try understanding others by active listening.

The basic belief that defines an optimistic businessperson is that setbacks or failures are due to circumstances, not some unchangeable problem with yourself.

Establishing a philosophy of hope will help defeat, depression and anxiety. Hope is a belief that you have the will and that you will find the way to accomplish your goal.

An optimistic outlook can be developed by practicing the belief that any setback is temporary, which requires project adjustment.

One characteristic of particular relevance in analyzing an individual's capability is whether a person acts or views himself/herself as a patrician aristocratic (noble or princely) or plebian (common). The reason why this viewpoint is relevant is that the treatment and consideration of others by any individual are influenced by the individual's viewpoint.

Self-reliance will lead to victory.

Cognitive restructuring means substituting positive thoughts for negative thoughts. Positive thinking and visualizing are used by champions.

If your attitude requires an adjustment, then some useful techniques to improve your attitude are:

- Look for humor in a negative situation
- Focus on successes, even small ones
- Simplify and ignore unimportant things

The influence mode of the rational mind is words. The influence mode of the emotional mind is non-verbal. Therefore, what is unsaid, but assumed, during a verbal communication can derail the communication. Remember to clarify and understand what is said.

A gem is not polished without rubbing. Steel is made by the application of fire. These principles apply to people, that means that people require friction and fire to shine and be strong.

People who cannot marshal some control over their emotional life fight inner battles that sabotage their ability for focused work and clear thought.[28]

The theory of multiple intelligence has evolved to focus on awareness of one's mental processes rather than on the full-range of emotional abilities.[29]

Emotional wisdom is gained through past experience. Reason without feeling is blind.[30]

Must blend the rational (cognitive) mind with the emotional for the greatest success and the most productive and happiest life.[31]

Sounder decisions result from being attuned to our feelings. This approach allows us to sort out the options.[32]

---

[28] Goleman, Daniel. *Emotional Intelligence.* New York: Bantam, 1997. P. 30.
[29] Goleman, Daniel. *Emotional Intelligence.* New York: Bantam, 1997. P. 41.
[30] Goleman, Daniel. *Emotional Intelligence.* New York: Bantam, 1997. P. 53.
[31] IBID
[32] Goleman, Daniel. *Emotional Intelligence.* New York: Bantam, 1997. P. 54.

Distinguish between what someone says or does and your own reactions and judgments.[33] An adversarial tone of conversation can prevent any progress.

American juries in litigation trials sometimes recommend awards based on emotional reaction, not on an unbiased evaluation of the facts of the case. This is one reason why awards are reduced during the appeal.

Everyone needs four types of energy. The amount of each of the four types that is applied to a situation needs to be adjusted. The four types are:
- Physical
- Mental
- Emotional
- Spiritual

"There is luxury in self-reproach. When we blame ourselves, we feel that no one else has a right to blame us." (Oscar Wilde)

"Eagles we see fly alone; and they are but sheep, which always herd together." (Sir Philip Sidney.) Therefore, it is OK to be a lone hunter and it is not necessary to follow the herd formed by everyone else. Think for yourself, but also be a cooperative team player.

What the superior man seeks is in himself, but what the small man seeks is in others. (Confucius) This means that we should seek to improve ourselves first.

Suffering becomes beautiful when anyone bears great calamity with cheerfulness, not through insensibility, but through greatness of mind. (Aristotle)

The brightest thunderbolt is elicited from the darkest storm. (Charles C. Colton) So, I interpret this statement to mean that power and strength develop from your dark days.

You are limited by your own attitude. Change your attitude about a variety of items such as people, projects, company, and you change your opportunities.

---

[33] Goleman, Daniel. *Emotional Intelligence.* New York: Bantam, 1997. P. 268.

Criticism should not hurt when it comes from the ignorant, uninformed, or complainer. Remember to apply this thought when confronted by criticism. You only need to consider constructive criticism from those you love, honor, or respect or those who love, honor or respect you.

Develop a counterbalance force by magnifying the positive when faced with negatives.

Engineering, particularly automotive, is goal oriented, other professions may not be. Therefore, when considering sales associates for the automotive industry whose background is not goal oriented, then you must realize that the individual may not be suitable.

"Men stumble over the truth from time to time …….. but hurry off as if nothing happened." (Sir Winston Churchill)

Contemplation is thinking with a purpose to resolve the issue.

We have authority and control over our lives. Therefore, when something happens to you, which is not to your liking, change it.

Anger blinds you to understanding.

Acceptance of authority, influence, and control allows understanding and an ability to work within the system.

Dead is quiet, alive is noisy. Therefore, do not just sit in quiet desperation, paralyzed by fear. Be alive, speak up, reach out, make mistakes and learn.

Take a risk and move toward what you want, or play it safe and choose comfort. People often choose comfort, although they do not realize that their comfort zone is protected by a wall of fear.

Do it, feel the fear, accomplish things, then you can bypass depression, and a feeling of being trapped.

Money is the Aladdin's lamp for many, this is what their dreams and freedom are made of.

How you deal with your enemies whether they be real or perceived, is an indication of the strength of your character.

Forgive and forget the personal and professional attacks on you. Do this for yourself.

When confronted with trouble or sadness, then recognize that tears are natural to healing and enjoying life.

It takes practice, patience, and discipline to be happy; but many people think that happiness comes from some special outside influence, and not something within themselves.

It has been reported that leaders require balance and focus in five areas:
1. Personal
   - Action oriented
   - Results oriented
   - Self-development
2. Interpersonal
   - Conflict resolution
   - Negotiation
   - Influencing
   - Oral communication
   - Writing
3. Employment
   - Coaching
   - Team leader
   - HR management
4. Business
   - Budgeting
   - Business knowledge
   - Creativity
   - Quality
   - Problem solving
   - Decision making
   - Planning and execution

5. Strategic
   - Vision
   - Change management
   - Technology management

You don't manage people; you manage projects but lead the people.

Liberal policies of tolerance can cause diversity of character but a worsening of social attitudes.

"Great minds discuss ideas, average minds discuss events, small minds discuss people."(Admiral Hyman Rickover, U.S. Navy)

Engineers tend to think in technical terms about product or process features. Leaders think in customer terms about benefits.

There is what the customer sees, and there is what company employees see. If these two visions are significantly different, then customer satisfaction will be negatively affected in the future.

Some people want to know the price of everything, but do not understand intrinsic value.

"It is much safer to obey than to rule." (Thomas Kempis). This belief contributes to situations where some people just complain rather than lead.

Avoid people who are constant cynics, they are poisonous.

Place yourself around people who are relaxed and balanced. Learn how they function and imitate their success.

Income inequality in China is less than in the U.S.[34] Long-term political and social stability requires containment of growing income inequality.

---

[34] Drucker, Peter. *Management.* New York: Harper and Row, 1973. P. 370

The significance of executive pay may be status, not income. Therefore, the money has changed from a basic need to an esteem need. This change can be better understood by studying the hierarchy concept of Abraham Maslow.

Establish your basic principles of personal conduct and values, but be open to refinements throughout life.

What matters more condition or conditioning? Neither, because both are equally important.

Develop a successful business attitude by developing your character and values.

Sometimes you may conceal your emotions in a mistaken belief that they will go away. Outwardly, you appear calm; but inwardly you are in turmoil. It is necessary to acknowledge your emotions and develop ways to treat them.

A psychological defense mechanism called "reaction formation" means assuming a facade that displays the opposite emotion from the one actually felt.

Some experts claim a link between choking off anger and depression. Therefore, the emotion that is not acknowledged and dealt with becomes a hidden sore.

Many people who easily demonstrate anger or hostility are in positions of power. They have learned that they can use these displays to control others. Recognize this tactic so that their hostility is not damaging to your self-esteem. The attacker is on a power trip because he needs a fix.

Leaving a room or leaving a company in the face of anger are valid coping mechanisms to be considered.

The physical or psychological emptiness felt by a person can be attributed to a poor work environment.

Career and personal stress are interrelated. A significant change in one will influence the other.

It is important to recognize that improving knowledge and understanding are always an asset. The stronger your assets, the more capability you have to approach your life as you desire.

Some people are very intense regarding a particular topic such as a project or a belief. A recognition of this may allow you to consider and understand how to react to such a person.

Work to improve injustice in your family, company and country.

Does any church or business have a legitimate mandate to engage in confrontational activities in either the political arena or in your life? I think, yes, within limits because the application of authority without morals leads to abuse.

Their are many that would like to fire those judges, regulators, bureaucrats, etc, who behave unaccountably and whose decisions are counter to society needs. However, the system may not permit this due to the potential for censorship.

Many people inappropriately approach problems by first asking, "Who is at fault?" instead of asking, "What is the problem?"

Ichor – A celestial fluid running, instead of blood, in the veins of gods. Perhaps, some ichor runs in our veins or, if not, then may be we need a transfusion to become more spiritual.

When something is troubling you, then instead of concealing your feelings try telling someone you trust. You may be surprised to learn that they have been through something similar and can offer some advice or at least be a kind listener.

Humor helps fight stress – look for it in yourself, others and situations.

A good player on a weak team will end up with lower ratings, than a good player who is fortunate to be playing on a winning team. The relevance of this within business is that you may be quite excellent at work, while other team workers are poor. You or others may assume that you are poor just because the team is. Do not let this happen.

Sometimes it is beneficial for you to be like a child -- free and spontaneous; instead of, scheduled and programmed.

Maintain a healthy curiosity in many topics so that you develop reserve knowledge. You may need to call your reserves into action.

Often when something goes wrong, there is a tendency to be overwhelmed. This leads to mental paralysis, which results in inaction. One action item to help you overcome paralysis is to get advice from a person you respect.

Achievement and success are what you decide they are. You do not have to mimic or follow others.

Sometimes, people need to vent without repercussions. It seems that this controlled venting is more likely done by women than men.

Some employees harass others (verbally abusive). These people want to be in control of an environment where people are intentionally mistreated by them.

Indications of mental difficulty or depression are loss in the sense of joy in being alive, a sloppy appearance, and trouble concentrating.

A wide range of background knowledge is a big help in utilizing the breakthrough thinking technique. This philosophy is the basis for the Russian problem solving technique that relies on past inventions. The Russian technique is called Triz.

Keeping up with the many books and journal articles which discuss future technological developments is stimulating and provides the wide range of background knowledge necessary for breakthrough problem solving.

Concentrating on raw statistics without background knowledge that allows proper interpretation can lead you down the wrong path.

If a person likes to deal in facts, then this person may be very reluctant to give opinions.

Put on hold those ideas that are currently inconsistent with your character. Future developments may cause you to reconsider the idea.

Your vision for the future requires action to create the reality of your vision.

If all people believed and followed the same basic principles such as love, honor and respect, then our legal, social and economic activities would be principle based instead of rule based.

Currently in the developed world, it appears that many people are unwilling to lead a life of sacrifice and work in the hope of gaining future leisure.

Happiness requires a balance of work and personal life. However, the balancing point is unique to an individual and to the particular situation.

The establishment and maintenance of creativity requires the following:
- Freedom and quiet time
- Tools and education
- Metrics to track results
- Good communication
- Support from management
- Recognition from peers and management
- Multifunctional experience or wide background knowledge

One way to reduce the underclass is to stop accepting the situation without requiring responsible behavior, just like, one way to reduce under performers at work is to stop accepting and rewarding their behavior.

Many politicians have a vested interest in the government's ability to award handouts because this ability is helpful to the politician's career.

When you feel yourself becoming angry, then try to concentrate your attention on understanding the person or situation.

Self-evaluation, whether it is done by or by individuals, is a painful experience but necessary to begin dealing with the changes that are required.

Do not practice misguided compassion by not expecting responsible behavior from co-workers, family, and friends.

Defending a position when under attack can be confusing, stressful and lonely. However, this is OK because you may be right and you may receive recognition and reward or just a feeling of accomplishment.

One self-serving approach to win an argument is to demonize an individual, company, country, race, culture, etc. Recognize when someone takes this approach and counter their tactic with inquiry about facts.

A problem cannot be solved unless you know the desired results.

Success can bring feelings of anxiety because of the fear of increased responsibility.

Recognize that labels that you use to define people, places or things can be simplistic and misleading. Using the definition as an initial categorizing of something is helpful in processing information as long as you understand that the labeling is subject to refinement.

Teach values. The application of knowledge without the consideration of values can create unethical or immoral results.

Doctors, family, and friends will sometimes dismiss a person's pain as imaginary and/or exaggerated. This seems more likely with older patients. The dismissal may contribute to the complainant's increasing concentration on pain and sadness. Chronic stress and/or chronic illness can seem like an emotional roller coaster for the complainant because of the effect of dismissal.

People who contribute the most to a job may not be financially rewarded the most. However, personal satisfaction also has value and each person must decide the relative importance of money in his/her life.

I have heard people say that the Democratic Party assaults basic American values, while the Republican Party is the party of the rich and selfish. I think that both impressions are too simplistic, but may be a useful initial label that requires refinement.

Follow the 80/20 rule used at Kodak. It is OK to be right 80% of the time, if you act quickly.

Energize yourself by developing higher self-esteem.

If you are preoccupied with avoiding criticism and being perfect, then you may be extremely self-critical. Self-examination is useful to allow you to correct future actions, while constant self-criticism is defeating you because the concentration is on past events.

Develop your thoughts because tough times will eventually stop but tough people go on.

When it is necessary for you to face a surviving spouse or children, don't say, "If there is anything I can do, let me know." Take action; don't wait because if the person must ask you then it isn't worth it.

Anger increases as fear increases.

Maturing males want to prove themselves, which is a desirable characteristic for military service.

Arrogant behavior leads to greed, which leads to corruption.

The Taft Hartley Act provided for an injunction of 80 days to resolve strikes that affect health/safety. (Note: I emphasized this act to state agencies when hospital nurses went on strike and my wife was awaiting a liver transplant. The nurses returned to work within two days.)

Big and fast wins the game, but small and thoughtful plans the game.

Having suffered from depression, I agree with the experts that the potential influencing factors can involve the nature and nurture of yourself. Both can influence your interpretations of life's events.

At various stages in my life, particularly, when overworked and/or facing spousal medical problems, I have felt exhausted, worthless, and hopeless. Only after several years did I realize that this was depression and could be treated.

Criticize others by pushing them down so that they can rise up. This is one tactic used by people is to help them maintain their superiority. Identify the tactic and use Tongue Fu to defend yourself from the verbal attack.

Groups will band together to fight the common enemy. This can be a tool to use by a leader to accomplish a difficult goal.

Education, motivation and self-interests are some of the items that can create valleys between the mountains of people. A leader's job is to build bridges between the mountains.

Some people, including me, struggle between self-awareness and self-destruction. You need to examine and understand yourself, but not to be overly critical of self. This can be accomplished by using problem solving techniques such as finding the root cause and developing an action plan so that your emphasis is future oriented, not past oriented.

A desirable work attitude can be developed and maintained by the following methods:
- Keep fit and rested
- An ability to work well with others because you have:
  - A positive outlook
  - An emphasis on fairness
  - Openness to ideas
  - A desire to solve problems
  - Alignment with organizational goals because you recognize that you succeed when your organization does.

People act as they feel, and they feel as they think. Therefore, positive thought processes result in more action because you are confident.

Sometimes you should consider changing jobs or careers so that your job is more properly aligned with your current priorities. Do not quietly stay where you are, living in misery.

As Homer said, "Here let us feast and to the feast be joined disclosure, the sweeter banquet of the mind."

Be a visionary for your operation and set high standards for the operation and the people. Close a potential loophole by holding people accountable.

The quality of your psychological self contributes to the quality of your material self.

A sin is not accompanied by a lifetime sentence unless you fail to recognize and correct the sin.

Trying is not a guarantee of success, but not trying is a guarantee of not being successful.

It is better to say that you are exploring the opportunities, instead of looking for a job, particularly when you are considering a job change.

Some people use hostile humor to boost themselves over other people. Their thinking is supported by a belief that person who is the recipient of hostile humor will not recognize the hostility or at least won't confront the behavior.

To have courage means to act now and overcome your fear.

Knowledge of what others do is interesting and can provide you with ideas. However, don't follow someone else, pursue your own dream.

A contributor to despair is a fear of death, but it is better to recognize that death is simply a returning home to God.

A country, company, or a person may have a feeling of being directed by a manifest destiny. This pursuit of their destiny can result in positive or negative consequences.

An appropriate acknowledgement of your anger is a necessary step to resolving conflict.

You need to develop on an emotional support system by forming associations with family, friends, coworkers, or an analyst.

Be careful about a knee jerk denial response. When confronted over an issue, then step back and consider what is being said before responding; otherwise, you may raise the level of conflict.

A combination of dreams and memories are important for balance. No dreams result in any energy, while no memory results in any direction.

Anger and *danger* are closely related.

Treat others with consideration. Actually, this is a variation of the Christian golden rule.

Nervousness is caused by focusing on your doubts and fears. Therefore, using positive visualization about how you will succeed will help you erase doubt and fear.

Face down your fears with visualization and transform doubts and fears into strength.

It is important to recognize that many individuals may indicate that something is common sense, but that does not mean it is common practice by the individual.

Hurt ages into anger. The following questions that you can ask of others to determine their intent may allow you to adjust your response.
- What do you suggest?
- How would you feel in this situation?
- What would you do in my place?
- What do you mean?

If you prefer to not ask a question, then remain silent and wait for the other person to add information.

People are usually more convinced by reasons that they partially discovered for themselves. Your discussion style should allow each individual to experience the discovery.

There are two concepts of rich: One is possession and the other is attitude. A person with a rich attitude has a higher value.

Your attitude makes the difference in every area of your life.

Some people never have happy todays because they focus on their unpleasant memories. Such people are unable or unwilling to replace memories with dreams.

A particular mistake you have made may reflect a decision or action in response to a particular situation. Do not allow this isolated mistake to define you.

Focus on what you have, not on what you don't have. Another way of saying this is -- to be happy where you are, not waiting to be happy until you arrive.

Some techniques that are used to develop and maintain a positive attitude are:
- Concentrate on positive factors that exist in your life.
- Change the way you look at work.
- Dreaming.
- Do not dwell on every decision. Move on and focus on the future.
- Do not give someone else power over you by dwelling on his/her opinions.
- Transfer a negative to the positive, then convert it to a goal.

Do not allow yourself to become over confident and arrogant. Laugh at your own self-importance. Interestingly, some religions preach that the self is not important, what is important is God and your devotion to God's teachings.

Asking questions during problem discussions with a coworker, customer or employee, can help resolution. Questions that are helpful are: How would you like me to respond to that? What can I do to help you? What evidence would convince you that is not true?

It has been said that it is easier to avoid a bad reputation than to overcome one. Hard working people seem to intuitively understand this.

Some people stubbornly hold on to beliefs, while other peoples' beliefs are easily changed. A more open minded approach is that you should search out and thoughtfully consider information and facts before forming a belief, but continue to listen to expressions of a different belief.

Our life is what our thoughts make it. Marcus Aurelius, a Roman emperor, made this insightful comment and yet violently persecuted Christians. Apparently, all was OK as long as the thoughts of others conformed to his.

What you see in your mind is what you create; what you think about is what you get and what you speak about is what you become. The meaning to this sentence is that your thoughts, actions, and speech must be aligned with your goals.

Forty thousand wishes won't fill your bucket with fishes. (Fisherman's saying) So, action must accompany thoughts. Proposals without action are inadequate.

The purpose of the following is to illustrate the multiple forces affecting a person:

External forces acting on a person are:
- Supervisor
- Peers
- Family
- Rules, norms and laws
- Circumstances

Internal forces acting on a person are:
- Self-image
- Needs and wants
- Desires
- Ability
- Values and interests

An Irish blessing states, "May your blessings outnumber the shamrocks that grow, and may trouble avoid you wherever you go." Sometimes I think about this Irish blessing and remember my good fortune.

Decision-making is by team, decision taking is by individual. This important distinction is sometimes missed. People may believe teamwork activity avoids individual responsibility but it does not.

A person may express negativism or pessimism as a response to an actual or perceived sense of being treated unfairly. If perceived, then it may be untrue. However, you may not be able to change someone's mind.
You are not a victim of life. So do not simply accept what comes your way.

A positive mental attitude requires:
- Faith
- Initiative
- Tolerance
- Tact
- Kindness
- Courage
- Generosity

If you concentrate on what you don't have, then you will never have.

Your thoughts and attitude create a powerful force for what you want.

There is a difference between self-survival, which is selfish based; and survival of self, which is integration based. This applies to:
- Nations
- Cities
- Companies
- Groups
- Neighborhoods
- People
- Families

People should take responsibility for themselves, but often do not.

There appears to be an erosion of civility in business and public life.

Be cautious about being too rigid in your thinking and actions and unaccommodating to change.

Chapter 4

Reflections on Business

Improve your business wisdom by understandings and careful consideration of the social, technical, spiritual, and psychological aspects.

Implementing change requires perseverance, wisdom, technology, and sometimes outside help.

Reengineering complements continuous improvement. Reengineering is needed when:
- Dramatic improvements are desired
- Market or customer demands have shifted dramatically

Reengineering is a radical redesign of a particular process to achieve dramatic improvements in speed, cost, quality, and service. Do not reengineer if a crisis exists or strategy does not exist.

Consider emphasizing the use of continuous improvement philosophy that will yield steady progress.

The progress of negotiations is better judged by the thoughtfulness of questions, not the length of time.

Employee exit interview questions should be prepared to obtain useful information. Questions about new opportunity, the reason for leaving, morale, and any suggestions can provide insight into your operation.

Management should be aware of certain definitions related to employee harassment such as a hostile environment. A hostile environment requires a continuing course of conduct, which is offensive and so pervasive that it interferes with a victim's ability to do their job. Generally, an isolated incident will not satisfy this definition.

If you wish to avoid hurting the feelings of others so that the problem solving session can be improved, then avoid judgmental language. Making a comment about what concerns you about the proposal without a personal attack will be an effective method to continue the discussion.

Many people forget that you cannot realize results without first realizing trying.

Courses of employee conduct that may be considered improper and detrimental to the organization are as follows:
- Misconduct (horseplay, stealing)
- Insubordination (not following rules, orders)
- Creating an undesirable working environment

Developing a can do attitude and aligning yourself with organizational goals are necessary even if self-employed.

Helpful hints on keeping your perspective at work are to use:[35]
- Self-control thru measurement
- Develop objective needs into personal goals
- Convert opportunities into results
- Remember that promotion is based on a factual record of performance, not potential
- Develop the personal sense of justice and decency
- Provide your full support of organizational objectives and priorities

Generally, managers are thought to have a broader outlook than non-management personnel. Managers should possess the ability to consider multiple viewpoints at the same time such as those of customer and company.

If you are faced with significant time constraints and are unable to accomplish all activities, then differentiate between your tasks and the common tasks. Complete your specific tasks first.

Most companies are organized by function that means communication, rewards, objectives and budget are organized by function. However, products and processes are cross-functional that causes functional conflicts. The problem solving process of cross-functional issues is not aligned with organizational structure, which makes it difficult to gain cooperation for problem solving.

---

[35] Drucker, Peter. *Management*. New York: Harper and Row, 1973 P. 441

Ineffective people create and prolong problems.

Setting goals is the manager's job.[36] Some managers avoid this responsibility because they fear employee complaints.

Management should provide for organized action with a can do attitude and alignment with organizational goals to be achieved by flexible employees.[37]

Peter Drucker says,

> "Every decision has two elements. What you really like to do? What you are able to do? The decision of which element to choose as the primary choice is influenced by politics and relationships." [38]

Several times in my career, I have been given responsibility without authority. This arrangement leads to weak unenforceable decisions and significant frustration.

A company must show through facts and data that it has a world-class management system, and is continually looking for ways to improve. This is a necessity to satisfy many quality and business operation standards such as QS-9000 and the Baldrige award.

When hiring someone, then focus on the candidate's behavior. How does the person think, act, and interact? Also, focus on chemistry. How does the person fit with the company's culture, team, dynamics, and management style? To be able to use such an approach requires that you define your company and group culture, its values and the group chemistry required.

Management can use stories to help employees learn about the company culture, how problems are solved and what traditions are held in respect. However, be careful! because some employees will misinterpret the purpose of the story as bragging, or unjust praise. Choose your words carefully to minimize this problem.

---

[36] Drucker, Peter. *Management.* New York: Harper and Row, 1973. P. 438
[37] IBID
[38] Drucker, Peter. *Management.* New York: Harper and Row, 1973.

It is possible to limit an employee from going to work for a competitor by using the following techniques:

- Require that each employee sign a no competition clause before being hired.
- Offer a buy-out package when the person quits. However, receipt of the money is contingent on signing a "no competition employment for 1-3 years at a competitor."

A person who has received training but lacks relevant experience may be denied promotions.

The worth of an office or company is the worth of the individuals composing it. This comment is similar to the comment that people are our most important asset.

The vast majority of effort in most companies relates to the creation, dissemination, and use of information. The determination of the added value of this effort requires an understanding of the whole needs of the enterprise.

When assigning an activity or project, then always explain the limitations of the delegate's authority. When receiving an activity or a project, ask or define the authority under which you will operate.

Time and resource management are essential components of good quality management of a business. In fact, these components are a consideration in quality awards such as ISO 9000, QS-9000 and Baldrige.

It is helpful to think of situations and change like a card game. During a particular hand some win, some lose, and some break even.

A manager needs to explain to employees that managing change is a discovery process. There is a broad overall plan with a goal in mind but unscheduled stops occur along the way resulting in delays or detours.

It is useful to remember that deeper trouble may occur if an organization does not change.

Assuming that the requirements of a company or a job are changing, then you probably need to be changing. For example, a change in culture or work pace may require you to acquire new knowledge.

Survival of the organization requires that each person support the organization. However, you should realize that the intention of the organization is to survive with or without your support. Those who withhold their support may be eliminated.

Establish your business and departmental priorities, then establish measurements to monitor the performance.

An organization can develop around self-generating processes, but will eventually require re-organization.

It is mandatory to have periodic management reviews to determine the adequacy of the business system. The review is necessary to determine the need and change in policies, philosophy, directives or methods.

Priorities are set by higher-level personnel, and customer objectives are understood and developed by lower-level personnel.

Customer and supplier relationships influence the success of both. Tread lightly for fear of breaking this bond.

As organizations downsize, the opportunities for organizational success decrease. Therefore, a well-thought-out business operational strategy is necessary for survival and to set the stage for future renewal of the organization.

Economic value is provided by proper utilization of assets, including employees. Value added is not simply measured by sales dollars.

Decentralization of operations may allow your organization to take advantage of new technologies.

You cannot ignore the dynamics of the world economy because developments in other companies or regions of the world can have a significant influence on you. Seek constant information to develop and maintain a world economy mind.

Each person should be offered professional respect, especially, for his/her different technical know-how.

Employees become more organization oriented when appropriate vision and goals are established by management. Then managerial duties include:
- Budgeting
- Evaluating and correcting
- Individual and organizational performance
- Goal setting
- Task follow-up
- Work scheduling
- Reporting progress
- Providing technical guidance
- Interpreting and insuring compliance with the organizations operating procedures and values
- Provide inspiration, motivation and development of employees
- Problem solving

Perform a gap analysis to determine the gap between where you are and where you want to be, before you determine any actions.

An employee who maintains a sharing and caring attitude towards others may suffer because of the vulnerability that the attitude creates. This problem can become a significant dilemma if the person is promoted to management and does not learn how to decrease his/her vulnerability.

Pick and choose your battles and battlegrounds carefully because the victor is determined based on which battles are won.

Companies are likely to have periods of great strength followed by periods of regrouping and refocusing. This pattern is likely because when operations are going well, there is a tendency to leave well enough alone. Unfortunately, while the company is performing well, it may also be using its reserve energy leaving a spent organization.

When an organization or a manager operates under a mantra of low trust and low understanding, then it is quite likely that the employees will suffer low spirit.

As business conditions change, then budget plan changes are required. It is not always possible to anticipate and plan for all possibilities.

It is sometimes necessary to regain control in a meeting. Two questions that can be used to regain control are:

- Can I interrupt you for a minute?
- You seem to have a problem with this! How would you fix it?

You cannot fully satisfy everyone. Trying to fully satisfy everyone will not satisfy yourself because you will be living in silent misery.

A leader is a teacher of others, not a doer for others.

It is necessary to hold people accountable for the improvement of activities within their area.

Business culture is defined by a combination of the following items:

- Results required by the organization
- Key measures used
- Key business drivers
- Formal and informal infrastructure and organizational practices
- Leadership practices
- Technology used
- Perception by employees, customers, suppliers and competitors
- History of the organization

Manufacturing processes/products can be

- Technology intensive. If so, then being close to the market allows quick market action.
- Labor intensive. If so, then being close to a source of low cost labor allows cost efficiency.

Where there is little production differentiation based on the price or on the core product, technology, then you must differentiate your company or your product by providing one or more of the following:
- Better product assortment
- Better service
- Greater customization of the product for specific customers
- Faster delivery
- Better quality
- Future technology improvements in design and/or manufacture

Three low cost methods to grow company profits are:
- Remove wasteful activity
- Establish good inventory practice, consistent with your customer needs
- Standardize procedures

However, be careful because of a potential negative impact on growing sales.

Some important skills that are required when developing a quality business operating system are:
- Communicating with others
- Building awareness and sharing of information
- Examination and improvement of how processes work together

"Controls have to be appropriate to the character and nature of the phenomena measured."[39] "Measurements have to be congruent with the events measured."[40]

Concepts that were introduced to me while I was reading P. Drucker's book on *Management*[41] are as follows:
- Management by objectives
- Self-control
- Converting objective needs into personal goals

The requirements of a good decision involve consideration of the following questions:
- Who has to know about it?
- What action is required?
- Who will take the action?
- What supporting actions are required?

---

[39] Drucker, Peter. *Management*. New York: Harper and Row, 1973. P. 500
[40] Drucker, Peter. *Management*. New York: Harper and Row, 1973. P. 501
[41] Drucker, Peter. *Management*. New York: Harper and Row, 1973.

Many issues in business are interwoven; therefore, a specific action being considered to improve one issue may have a ripple effect on other issues. You think about the impact of actions on your business, before you jump.

The establishment of goals requires that organizational goals precede departmental goals, which precede individual goals. This process can occur formally which is the best approach or informally wherein the manager prepares the organizational goals, as he understands them.

A manager may cluster responsibilities within people or department. This approach simplifies coordination but does not improve interdepartmental understanding.

A recent emphasis is on agile manufacturing that is really quick response. Quick response requires flexibility, cooperation, and organization.

A manager's job involves two-way communication involving carrying information and ideas down and up the organization.

Undertake challenges that are believed to be within the capabilities of the person. However, recognize if the challenges prove tougher than expected and provide assistance.

Upfront planning builds a project information base to help direct the overall design and implementation of the project.

Flowcharting the process steps in office or manufacturing operation will identify bottleneck or redundant areas.

Sales personnel are fond of saying that the customer or market caused the problems. This is acceptable providing information is provided on potential tools and alternatives to improve the situation.

It is your duty to find full or partial solutions while operating within the business culture.

Management wisdom begins with recognizing the value of trust in your relationship with employees and customers.

Leaders that do not lead by personal example and style cannot expect employees to go where they won't.

Adam Smith said that government was needed to educate the labor force, assure economic infrastructure, and maintain public safety. The rest should be left up to the market. However, in todays global marketplace the consideration of an economic infrastructure cannot be limited to one's home country.

Articulation of a simple, compelling vision is the task of leader. Leaders inspire others to boldly go where no one has gone before.

Business process and business strategy should be aligned by:
- Focusing on results, not activities
- Leveraging information technology as an enabler of your employees. A tool to use.
- Practicing continuous improvement
- Improving business practices before reinforcing them with heavy investments in technology

Greed and office politics can overcome friendship and loyalty in the workplace. I received this message from the 1994 movie "Disclosure".

Eliminate confusion, waste, and finger pointing. Institute responsibility, accountability, and methods of problem solving.

Interesting questions to ask your employees are:
- "What do we mean by success in our business?" and
- "How do the process support customer needs?"

The answers you receive will reveal the quality of your strategic communication, and may help identify new focuses.

Business objectives are like airline flight schedules and plans, necessary, but adjustable depending on conditions.

A manager's job is to set priorities, make decisions, and take responsibility for the outcome. However, some employees may incorrectly believe that they are not required to make recommendations and are not responsible for the outcome as well.
The desire for power to influence others makes a great manager.

Alignment of activities at the department level is difficult without a consistent organizational mission or values.

Lack of marketing ability with a lack of new technologies is a deadly problem. Any significant change in standards, mission or responsibilities requires the acquisition of new resources. This applies to individuals and to corporations.

Rushing into markets is not a recipe for success. Background knowledge of the market needs and values is required.

Improvement in productivity should accompany an increase in production capacity.

Companies regain market share by focusing on customer service and support, product lines, pricing distribution networks, and lower capital expenditures.

A little extra effort or extra time may be the difference between ordinary and extra ordinary.

Get rid of resources that do not improve your competitiveness and expand areas that add value. Be careful to align your value with your customer.

Personal attributes of those who are successful in business are:
- Adding value in the performance of each job
- Creating change and continuous improvement
- Being a self-starter
- Recognizing and seizing opportunities
- Demonstrating leadership
- Practicing lifelong learning

Manage your own career and maintain contacts.[42]

Research conducted at Boston University determined that when you are in charge, you have not only the power, but also the obligation to make the rules. You must motivate people to achieve.

---

[42] Kotter, John P. *The New Rules.*

Dramatic economic change fuels social instability. This effect is most often noticed in countries but also applies to companies.

National security or insecurity is better defined in economic terms.

Individuals who are well connected in the industry can be an asset to your business; however, the individual needs to offer something tangible besides social contact.

Conflict may or may not require intervention. Recognize that personal conflict is animosity that involves deeply rooted opinions and attitudes, while substantive conflict involves perceived differences about actual data or facts.

Conflict resolution requires that the parties:
- Focus on issues
- Be conscious of
  - Differences over facts. This may seem unusual because facts are gathered but facts are also interpreted to create a belief.
  - Differences over goals
  - Differences over methods
  - Differences over values. This particular item can influence the other three causing apparent disagreements. However, the real root cause of the conflict is a value difference, perhaps, due to a cultural difference.

Critical success behaviors for individuals are:
- Oriented toward goal achievement
- Maintaining a positive outlook
- Ability to organize action
- Informed risk taking
- Flexible thinking combined with a problem solving desire

A good rule of thumb is to localize production close to markets. There are notable exceptions to this rule such as high labor content products (an example is footwear).

The purpose of a business is to create and keep a happy customer. This goal never changes, only the strategy to achieve it.

Companies must offer better value for the money realizing that technology is fleeting; so, consistent improvement is necessary.

Issues, which are complicated and volatile, are more susceptible to a miscalculation and conflict. Therefore, use the conflict resolution items mentioned earlier.

A decisive strategist, tenacious change agent, and an inspiring communicator are characteristics of a turnaround leader.

Oftentimes the largest volume of customers for a product has strict cost goals and do not want unnecessary options. This market segment may not represent the highest possible profit margin, but does represent the highest dollar volume.

The farther your design center is from your customers, the worse your products will be. This is true because the design center will not understand the customer.

Work to the agenda of customers, not the agenda of a plant or a corporation. You must produce what a customer wants, at the price he is willing to pay.

The trend in manufacturing is to either have distributed physical facilities at the point of consumption or use express order and delivery.

The most cost efficient system is one that will turn out the product the customer wants in the quantity the customer ordered, with zero inventory with a manufacturing location close to the customer.

When individuals or companies dismiss ideas or trends because of the not invented here philosophy, then they are blinded by the use of selective intelligence.

Organizational stress causes inefficiency, while creative tension results in better solutions.

Allocate space to employees based on need, not title.

Union leaders should remember that unions do not create jobs, customer need creates jobs.

Quality, manufacturing, engineering and general office work requires that a multifunction collective approach to work be used, rather than a lone wolf approach that is generally favored by sales personnel.

People may wonder why they need to change. The answer is that situations change due to changes in technology, legal, economic, political, and social factors.

A destructive tendency in negotiations is a desire to top the other person. Better to realize that to win it may be necessary to appear to lose.

The mark of a successful organization is not problems corrected, but problems repeated.

People have a tendency to form and voice opinions based on unspoken assumptions and insufficient information.

Sexual harassment requires evidence of:
- Being propositioned
- An atmosphere of hostility, unwelcome, abusive, or discriminatory behavior
- The creation of fear of losing your job, if you do not participate
- Complaints to upper management

Improvement plans require that top management is 100% behind you and visibly supporting your effort.

Aggressively challenge and manage consultants, when you use their services.

Causes of stress and reduced loyalty in the workplace are:
- High job demands
- Low skill and low authority, typically in high control hierarchical organizations

Change your thinking from managing, organizing, and controlling to providing vision, value, and mental models.

Healthy skepticism applied to organizational performance problems can develop into a corrosive cynicism, especially when problems continually reoccur.

Leaders lead by example, devotion, enthusiasm, comments, work, reports, dress, action, and interest.

When considering hiring, promoting, or reassigning an employee, then consider, how well the individuals characteristics, skills, and qualities from Table 1, which follows, match the job requirements.

Table 1[43]
Performance Factors

Intellectual Characteristics

Intelligence	Memory	Ability to learn
Curiosity	Analytical ability	Quick thinking
Creativity	Rationality	Systematic decision making

Personal Qualities

Innovativeness	Honesty	Enthusiasm
Self-confidence	Resourcefulness	High energy
Adaptability to change	Positive attitude	Sense of urgency
Risk taking	Persistence	Good humor
Emotional maturity		

Interpersonal Skills

Openness to criticism	Admits errors	Friendly
Expressiveness	Competitiveness	Empathy
Defuses anger	Humility	Emotional control
Patience		

Communication Skills

Writing	Speaking	Listening
Reading	Signing	

Leadership Qualities

Vision	Decisiveness	Applauds others
Professionalism	Tolerance of individuality	Conflict resolution skills
Meeting leadership skills	Accept ideas of others	Results oriented
Ability to teach		

---

[43] Deep, Sam and Sussman Lyle. *Smart Moves for People in Change*. Reading, MA: Addison Weekly, 1995. P. 143-144

Low tolerance for mediocrity	Inspirational	Earns respect

Follower Qualities

Meeting participation skills	Reliability	Works without supervision
Enjoys serving customers	Team player	Loyalty
Acceptance of authority	Trustworthiness	

Technical Skills

Precision	Awareness of field	Knowledge of new developments
Technical competence	Physical capability for demands	Proven track record

Criticism can have a beneficial effect by stirring you to fight and achieve something beyond what you normally would.

Prioritize the major demands on your time, such as:
- Crisis items (emergencies only you can handle)
- Direction items (planning activity)
- Routine maintenance (tasks which are regular or planned)
- R & R (refresh yourself)

The function of a meeting is oftentimes to generate discussion. Occasionally, the meeting is F.Y.I. (For Your Information). You need to be clear on the purpose of the meeting before the meeting begins.

Workers should be expected to behave with courtesy and respect; this includes no criticism and complaints to third parties.

A workplace should involve harmony, balance and unity.

A leader prepares a structure for cooperation.

Financial crisis also develops into social and political crisis.

Effective development and marketing strategy can stimulate demand.

Stay in winning shape by continually redefining what you are.

Chapter 5

The Consideration of Quality

Important qualities of employees are:
- Sense of mission
- Enthusiasm
- Ability to focus on goals
- Awareness that consensus is strength
- Faith in self

Note: Management can assist employees to become stars by providing assistance in identifying missions, challenges, and goals.

QS-9000 is a management system to design and maintain quality throughout all facets of the organization. Therefore, document not only the quality system, but also the business process.

It is has been written that there are six causes of quality problems:
- Lack of organization
- Lack of training
- Lack of discipline
- Lack of resources
- Lack of time
- Lack of top management support

Incompetent and ill-trained personnel in the auditing and quality assurance areas will cause the quality business system to fall into disrepute.

Defensive behavior is from defensive reasoning. Productive reasoning is required for quality teamwork. People who exhibit defensive reasoning tend to:
- Be closed minded and conclusive in interactions
- Be confrontational, not confrontable
- Do not provide valid data, but state vigorously their opinions

Quality begins with having the right people. The right people possess team skills and an ability to view problem resolution from a systems perspective.

Many organizations do not document their operations because of a mistaken belief that spontaneous problem solving would be reduced. The organization does not understand that you must be able to determine the problem and measure the problem using the document map. Preparing a document map also helps to anticipate other problems and take steps to prevent the problem.

Are procedures and documents of the quality or business system known, available, and used by personnel? If the answer to this questions is "no", then training and usage enforcement are required.

Robert Kelly lists employee star qualities as the following:[44]
- Initiative
- Networking
- Self-management
- Perspective
- Followership
- Leadership
- Teamwork
- Organizational savvy
- Persuasion skills

The quality department does not own quality. Each person and department has to take responsibility for the quality of its own work. The quality department provides expertise and advice.

Some key components of successful organizational change are:
- Leadership
- Cultural change
- Workforce involvement
- Communication and measurement
- Education
- Supportive human resources
- Shared sense of urgency among employees
- Lifelong learning ideal among employees

---

[44] Kelly, Robert E. *How To Be A Star At Work.* New York: Times Books, 1998

During a review of your operations by an outside auditor such as would occur with an ISO 9000 or QS-9000 audit, it is an absolute requirement to record objective evidence of the system by an auditor. Evidence is collected from:

- Interviews
- Examination of documents
- Observation of activity

An audit of your business process, which is conducted by either internal or external auditors, will consider your processes using the following criteria:

- Suitable for operation
- Conformance of standards
- Effectiveness

Motivating corrective action is a major objective of all quality business audits.

A quality auditor must be knowledgeable in various areas such as quality, reliability, auditing, and maintainability of a business system.

Every work task includes four elements:

- Persons (those who perform and supervise)
- Item (product, document, etc.)
- Equipment (tools etc.)
- Information (drawing, specification, data)

Therefore, when you are preparing work instructions make sure that each element is clearly identified.

It is sometimes required to remove a person to solve a problem.

Everyone should be involved in determining if you are meeting customer expectations and needs. This can be accomplished by formal or informal surveys, site visits, or field performance measurements.

When you are reviewing a quality system, a process or just a report, do not assume that personnel possess a high level of competence and knowledge. Look for evidence and attitude.

The acid test of the system is the product. So, field performance is an acid indicator of whether you are meeting customer needs. Unfortunately, this information is after the fact and so needs to be combined with earlier indicators.

Constant revisions to a process or system may signal that the basic system is poor and that there is a serious quality problem requiring greater attention.

Operational audits are a critical examination for completeness and correctness.

The allocation, use and monitoring of resources are a basic requirement for business success since it affects quality and operations.

A quality product results from a defined and monitored sequence of activities.

Analysis is the conversion of raw data into useful information. You should expect employees to collect data and provide some analysis. One type of analysis involves the organization of data in a manner that reveals patterns such as time or location sensitivity.

Quality cost information, which is useful in the determination of whether operations are satisfactory, can be provided in monetary equivalents. (% yield, # of errors, rework hours, etc.)

Do not select nitpickers to be a business, quality or process auditor. These individuals are often unreasonable and uncompromising.

Internal or external auditors should refrain from dramatizing or exaggerating a situation, especially, when reporting to management.

There are always minimum of two parts to problem solutions:
- Action
- Continued verification

In todays environment there are various state, national, and international quality awards. Receiving an award is a desirable achievement. However, your chances of receiving the award are improved if you recognize and encourage the continuation of that learning that occurs during the process.

Quality is required from everyone. This requires that people develop a quality mind, which means apply themselves, be creative, cooperate, stop finger pointing, and be involved. Those companies that are staffed with such individuals, top to bottom will thrive.

"Pursue process perfection" is a basic tenet of continuous improvements. (Kaizen)

Automobile dealers have a financial incentive to replace parts. Therefore, warranty data analysis should focus on customer complaints.

Set expectations for benchmarking activities and document the process before you begin.

Benchmarking partners could be best competitors, or functional industry leaders.

Many organizations will only react to problems, which are generally considered the firefighting mode. Anticipatory problem solving is required by the market place.

When judging best practices, it is essential to find those organizations that perform the activity as the core of their business. Benchmarking those organizations will provide helpful information.

Reviewing potential improvements requires detailed information, not just opinions.

Change from a philosophy of correction to one of prevention.

In business it is preferable to standardize some reports. The standards for form and content enhance the reading and understanding of the information, but do not severely limit the author's creativity.

It is beneficial to periodically schedule a management review of the business operating system. This review allows management to take a step back and consider the adequacy of the system and to make any changes in policy, philosophy, directions or methods.

When you are reviewing an operation, you need to balance the search for facts with consideration of people and situations.

Certification of your business quality operating system by independent audit is not a guarantee that the business will be successful. However, achievement and maintenance of certification can contribute to success.

A product or report may satisfy the letter of the law (a standard), but not the intent. You should consider how you could satisfy the requirements and the expectations (intent).

Your career success depends on your developing capability to conduct productive meetings, lead problem solving discussions, and to mediate and manage personnel or personality differences.

You need to consider the value contribution of each step in a process.

Focus on the process of improvement, which is to create something better, not perfect.

Data can bury you in so much detail that you lose sight of the objective. This is similar to the spread of an infection in your body and so can appropriately be called dataitis.

Keys to success in the initiation and ongoing motivation of quality programs are:
- Senior management support
- Having the right team members
- Having a good facilitator

Implement effective partnerships with customers by providing service or support deemed of value by customers.

Your participation in diverse groups will broaden your knowledge and contribute to opportunities for success.

Cross-functional discussions improve operating systems because the system that all must use was developed by all.

People in technical fields should be knowledgeable in quality, reliability, accounting, industrial engineering, computers, psychology, and sociology/legal issues.

A good manager should have the following basic characteristics:

- Respect for individuals and their potential
- A desire to manage by fact
- A desire to pursue continuous improvement
- A desire to organize for customer intimacy and satisfaction

There is a link between Internet abuse, data accumulation, and information addiction. (Dataitis)

As Om Gupta, a quality specialist, has said that you should stop focusing on a quality system, but should be focusing on the quality culture.

The benefits of having your business quality operating system certified to a national or international standard are:

- Your business is built on a solid foundation
- Increases the comfort level of current or future customers
- Independent recognition of a quality standard, which is essentially best practice

If you are using design reviews, then you should consider the following items:

- Cost – timing – manufacturing equipment and analysis
- Delivery requirements
- Environment testing
- Drawings or specifications
- Special testing
- Customer requirements
- Communication issues

A design review guideline, which I prepared while employed by a major supplier to the automotive industry, is provided as an example on the following pages. An example of a new technology review format, which I have also used and which provided lively discussion and insight is also provided.

Outline

    A.   **Purpose**

    B.   **Design Review Content**

    C.   **Meeting Format**

    D.   **Timing**

    E.   **Participants**

A.   **Purpose**

The intent of the design review process is to provide for the qualitative and quantitative examination of a proposed design to insure that it is manufacturable, meets the intent of appropriate "Specification for Engineering Designs (SED), is reliable during use, is cost effective and satisfies customer objectives. Good designs are a prerequisite for good quality, and the design review process is an effective method to prevent chronic quality programs.

B.   **Design Review Content**

The following material is to be presented and discussed during the design review meetings (see section D for specifics):

1. System and design content, including customer expectations and alternative approaches.

2. Conformance to applicable standard design principles:

    a) Specification for engineering design
    b) S.A.E.
    c) A.S.T.M.
    d) Supplier design criteria
    e) Customer design criteria
    f) Producibility checklist

3. Engineering and quality characteristics relationship to customer expectations or functional requirements. Optional techniques to be used to establish this relationship are: Quality Function Deployment (QFD), quality/counterpart characteristics matrix, or a thorough customer/engineer/quality product/process analysis.

4. Reliability prediction using reliability block diagrams.

5. Cost, weight, and timing estimates for the production program, including suppliers and testing labs.

6. Cost and timing estimates for the prototype program.

7. Engineering specification proposal with reference to applicable Design Verification Specification Listing.

8. Design FMEA status.

9. Process FMEA status.

10. Circuit analysis and tolerance stacks.

11. Drawing release estimates.

12. Process capability studies – components.

13. Process capability studies – assembly.

14. Process capability studies – system factors.

15. Design verification plan and report – laboratory analysis.

16. Design verification plan and report status – vehicle testing.

17. Failure analysis of lab and vehicle test parts, including cause and effect analysis.

18. Reliability performance as measured by testing and construction of suitable reliability growth measurement (DUANE, AMSAA).

19. Source selection review (suppliers).

20. Packaging review (damage assessment):
   a) Components
   b) Finished assembly

C. Meeting Format

All relevant factors as listed in the Design Review Content section of this specification are to be addressed. A structured format with a specific agenda is an essential element of the design review, and will be followed to insure continuity and completeness. The core issue to be determined is whether we are or are not meeting program objectives. A concise statement of the major issues is to be included as the coversheet of each design review report. Additional material is to be attached to the summary sheet, which provides the basis for the summary assessment. This approach increases the focus of design and development efforts on the major problems to assure a satisfactory resolution within timing deadlines.

D. Timing

Design reviews are to be scheduled per the following timetable:

1. At concept stage, prior to cutting prototype tooling (phase I). Areas to be reported include:

   a) Concept

   b) Conformance to standards

   c) Expectations to characteristics (functional)

   d) Reliability prediction

   e) Design FMEA

2. At originally scheduled conclusion of phase II prototype testing ($\pm$ 2 weeks), even if testing is not on schedule. (Note: Phase II prototypes are defined as sample size larger than concept units (phase I) which

were built to determine the limits of product performance for the intended application.) Areas to be reported on include all items from design review number 1 plus the following:

a) Production cost estimate

b) Production weight estimate

c) Production timing estimate

d) Prototype timing estimate

e) Engineering specification

f) Process FMEA

g) Circuit analysis/tolerance stack

h) Drawing release

i) Capability studies

j) Design verification plan and report status (DVP&R)

k) Failure analysis/corrective action plan

l) Reliability growth

3. At originally schedule internal I.S.I.R. ($\pm$ 2 weeks). All areas to be reported on.

4. Four (4) to six (6) months after production shipments begin. An additional item of early quality indicators – field data is to be reported on.

5. Design reviews are to be scheduled yearly for all existing production designs. The initiation of the "full" design review sequence is advised whenever major changes in fit/form/function occur on an existing product line.

E.   Participants

The following chart lists probable participants and responsibility:

Participants	Responsibility
Chairperson (Engineering manager or designate)	- Calls, conducts meeting. Functions as moderator, critiques input during and afterwards.
Design Engineer of Product	- Prepares and presents design and substantiates decisions with data from tests or calculations. Critiques input during and after meeting.
Reliability or Quality Engineer	- Evaluates design for optimum reliability relative to goals. - Review and comment on inspection control and test frequency/methods.
Purchasing	- Assure that acceptable parts and materials are available to meet cost/delivery schedules. - Suppliers selected, surveyed methods.
Engineering Services -	- Review and comment on test plan, accept/reject criteria. Test environment, plan dates and test duration, test equipment/fixture availability.

Manufacturing Engineer (responsible for all prototype assembly, production tooling and material flow)	- Review and comment on manufacturability
	  - Fastening technology
	  - Sealing technology
	  - Assembly technology
	  - Inspection and feedback control

Sales	- Review and comment on satisfaction of customer requirements (price, timing, delivery, test)

A review format that has been issued when considering the application of a new technology application is as follows:

- Application

- Potential customers

- Competitors (current and future)

- Market potential within five years

- Selling price

- Technology availability at suppliers

- Functional basics

- Prototype costs

- Confidence in design/manufacture/business potential

- Competing technologies

- Timetable for decisions/parts

- Substantiation and references

- Expected reliability (model)

- Interface design compatibility potential system influence

- Relationship of technical performance to cost and schedule performance

- Resource requirement and availability

- Regulatory influence

A manufacturing plant's activity can be categorized into five basic functions:
- Working operation
- Inspection or measurement
- Materials handling
- Assembly and packaging
- Central control

Maintaining a spirit of continuous improvement requires motivation. A recognized standard to be satisfied or other corporate quality activity requirements can be used to provide this motivation.

The quality management of an organization requires involvement of many functions, such as administration, leadership, R&D, production, sales and marketing. It is necessary to consider the needs and expectations of all concerned parties when processes are involved.

The danger of not pursuing improvement is to risk stagnation. Stagnant water is foul from lack of motion.

If you are going to control a process, then you need to regularly measure the process or product. The measurements should satisfy the following seven attributes:
- Economical
- Meaningful
- Appropriate
- Congruent
- Timely
- Simple
- Operational

The scientific management application to a project will involve the following activities:
- Statement of objectives
- Collection of facts and data
- Breaking data into details
- Analysis
- Interpretation

Customize your business system just as you customize a house. Begin with a template, but modify the template to suit your needs.

Development of a strategy by an automotive industry supplier involves consideration of:
- How to move the supplier into the future
- The expectations of automotive customer companies involving supplier proficiencies
- Competition and flexibility on a world basis
- Potential new competitors
- World economics and interaction with politics and nationalism
- Developing non-traditional relationships

A simple straightforward goal is to develop and use the full potential of the organization. The satisfaction of this goal requires effort by everyone in the organization.

You should have a positive expectation in your ability to improve the entire enterprise and the security of its employees.

Companies must be careful not to create too much bureaucracy. Overly bureaucratic companies sap employee morale and erode initiative and effectiveness.

Variability in output of a process is often caused by variable input. For example: The output of an educational system is not constant or consistent because the inputs to the system i.e. teachers, students, books are variable.

When you perform an operations self-exam, then you are comparing yourself to an ideal standard.

It is important to recognize that an organization does not exist independently.

Management's job is to provide focus on common purpose. The processes and procedures developed will be in support of the common purpose.

A sound business management system begins with a world-class quality philosophy. An indication of a world-class quality philosophy should be found in the business plan.

As you review systems, people, and products, look for measurable progress. This requires discipline and commitment.

The understanding of the principles and techniques of quality management is a necessary part of the corporate growth process.

A dissatisfied customer does not mean something is broke. It could mean that customer expectations were not satisfied.

Process optimization requires an understanding of the relationship of each step in the process, and the relationship of the process to the system.

The quality of the information that you receive is influenced by the quality of the relationships you have.

Develop a process focus rather than simply focusing on the end result. In other words, emphasize quality of operations instead of just immediate sales.

The implementation of quality operating systems will provide the framework for a business to build on.

The benefit of using recognized quality and business standards, as an organizing principle, is the improved business processes and customer satisfaction that will occur and not just the receipt of a certificate.

The effectiveness of an improvement process is as strong as the weakest link in the process. Your job is to identify the weak link and strengthen.

An evaluation of various industry segments is useful in the identification and analysis of existing or past method.

Recognize that the quality of your operation involves statistical as well as behavioral techniques.

A Change Leader leads by mentoring others.

Occasional "Creating Change" or "Suggestions for Improvement" meetings may be beneficial in soliciting opinions and comments from the organization.

Recognize that the manufacturing of a product requires the information driven enterprise. The enterprise has a great need for wide communication.

Potential goals to be considered by an organization are:
- Best in customer satisfaction
- Deliver financial – performance commitments
- Execute a restructuring plan
- Rechart the future (strategy)

Baseball and golf use metrics to determine how the team or individual is doing. Yet, many people in business resist the use of metrics for themselves.

Employees may not be able to adjust to changes on the fly and may resist any attempt at constructive criticism. Consider the addition of supportive internship, summer or contract help to provide inertia for change.

Do not view the implementation of quality standards as a quick fix. The philosophy of the standard must be integrated into the long-term business strategy.

The need for record keeping is as a historical foundation with which to build on the previous success.

The identification of the root cause of a problem is a necessary step in problem solving. The root cause must be controllable. If the cause is not controllable, then it is not a root cause.

Delegation of activities is necessary in the development of your people.

Become customer centered, not product centered.

Organizational agreement on business fundamentals will reduce conflict. Therefore, develop a stronger consensus on fundamental issues.

Build stronger customer relationships by providing supportive actions.

Good business requires good data.

Chapter 6

The Care and Understanding of People and Employees

Inadequate communications are common and severe problem in many businesses.

The delegation of a project requires that you provide:
- Desired results
- Guidelines
- Resources
- Consequences
- Standards to measure results versus expectations
- Control or review dates

The development of good relationships with others is dependent on understanding and acceptance of self.

Effective interaction between people requires respect between people.

Managers who tolerate poor performance because of a fear of confrontation are demotivating their entire staff. Therefore, managers should be familiar with the employee disciplinary activity process that involves the following steps:
- Feedback
- Coaching
- Oral reprimand
- Written reprimand
- Probation
- Temporary layoff
- Demotion
- Termination

Sending an employee home while an investigation of theft or other serious misconduct is conducted is a reasonable approach to consider.

Some people have plenty of excuses to support their lack of accomplishment.

When terminating an employee -- be decisive, direct, and nonconfrontational. Stick to the reasons for the decision.

Form natural work units by combining people into areas of similar interest.

Issues that cause personal conflict in organizations are:
- Lack of consistency in the treatment of employees
- Low trust between employees
- Inadequate respect
- Differences in facilities available to employees
- Differences in the dress requirements of employees
- Differences in the application of policies
- Differences in privileges granted to employees

Motivation is adversely affected by the following conditions, particularly, when there is a relative difference to others:
- Working conditions
- Obnoxious superiors
- Responsibility that is incompatible with authority
- Lack of career prospects
- Inadequate pay

Some job skills become less important due to advancing technology. Therefore, stop promoting only on the basis of a proven job skill. Personal initiative, individual accountability, and a focus on results are highly desirable traits to be considered for promotion.

A person who frequently changes jobs is said to have " a rich job history."

Develop flexible employees by creating clear and challenging goals.

A broad base of knowledge, skills, and culture is required to assume added responsibility.

When discussing problem behavior with an employee, ask what they can do to prevent the problem behavior.

Remember that the goal of constructive criticism is to instruct, correct, and improve performance by providing clear purpose and expectations. The goal is not to get even or find fault.

Leaders must encourage the people in their organization to develop skills and to satisfy performance objectives.

The company's performance management system requires data and analysis so that appropriate action plans can be developed.

As I understand, the American with Disabilities Act (ADA), employers may not have a duty to accommodate conditions that are controlled by medication.

Continued disloyalty by an employee, evidenced by remarks critical of the company, management, or staff, requires disciplinary action because of the following potential problems:
- Hurts teamwork
- Shows lack of commitment
- Shows lack of respect which undermines company or management effectiveness
- Damages overall morale

Constant complaining may represent a person's character or particular style. A constant complainer may retain his/her mindset, but he/she should be stopped from expressing it at work.

Managers must make it clear that unjustified comments of unfairness or mistreatment will not be tolerated.

More severe discipline can be applied between similar incidents providing justification is available. Ideally, justification is supported by documentation, situational difference, difference in severity, job responsibility differences, or job history.

Evidence of an attempt to correct the behavior of an employee can be provided by a letter to the employee that states:

- Unacceptable behavior
- The impact of such behavior
- Specific changes required
- An outline of the consequences
- A plan for improvement required and implemented

A rumor of employee substance abuse, harassment, theft, etc. are allegations, not hard facts. An investigation, including interviews, is required before any decision is made.

Reports of harassment require prompt action by the company.

Fear of violence in a workplace is as disruptive as the actual violence. Management needs to correct disruptions caused by any employee that uses intimidation or threatening behavior.

The primary objective of a performance review is to improve performance, not get it over with and not a feel good only discussion.

The fate of some employees is disproportionately important to the fate of the organization, and may be used as justification for pay increases. However, this should be fact based, not opinion based.

Less severe punishment may be administered to a lower-ranking employee than to a higher-ranking employee if both were involved in a violation of the same rule.

A protected characteristic such as a disability does not mean that the person can act with indifference to the rules of the organization.

No law requires employers to hire applicants who cannot do the job, whether they are disabled or not.

The purpose of the disability law is to provide equal opportunity, not charity.

It is easy to trust people who consistently do their best and/or live up to the their commitments. It may be said that such people are reliable, honest, motivated, enthusiastic, cooperative, or respectful.

Each person is accountable for the results of his/her decision and actions. A company is only as good as the people who represent it.

Disciplinary sessions with a disruptive employee should seek the employee's viewpoint about why things are not working.

To change a habit requires work and action.

Organizational rules are necessary but unnecessary rules are a demotivator for employees and unenforced rules contribute to employee contempt.

When we feel uncomfortable long enough, we begin to feel discouraged.

"A problem is a challenge to do your best." (Duke Ellington)

When considering a person for employment or promotion, one should consider goals achieved and challenges overcame in different situations including work and nonwork.

An employee performance agreement needs to outline the expectations to be satisfied. The expectations can include:
- Required results
- Guidelines on the required activity such as:
    - Recommend actions
    - Act and report immediately
    - Act and report periodically
    - Act on your own
    - The criteria indicating accomplishment

A managerial dilemma is reflected in the following dichotomy:
- Manager wants more for less
- Employee wants more for less

The solution to this dichotomy is to achieve agreement on performance and potential rewards.

Employees who work at improving their competence with the tools and processes of total quality should be provided encouragement and respect.

Promotion decisions should be based on a consideration of the following factors:
- Technical skills
- People skills
- Current organizational needs
- Future organizational needs
- Past performance
- Seniority
- Diversity needs
- The interest of the individual being considered
- Ability
- Attitude
- Cooperation
- Results achieved

Design a system of measures and rewards that adjusts to employees.

Feelings of friendly behavior vs. sexual harassment are influenced by the attitudes of the individuals involved. However, the determination by the organization is based on societal norms, not what is normal for the particular individual involved.

A dream will become a goal when you begin to apply energy.

The manager should understand the big picture of the company's mission and how each employee supports the mission.

Justifiable privileges may be associated with particular job positions within an organization. This is not elitism but only a recognition of differences.

Be flexible and take on new tasks.

Take the initiative to resolve problems.

Understand the company business.

Employee empowerment is not achieved by abandonment. A structure is required.

A change in employee compensation should be considered when you revise responsibilities. The sooner pay is changed, after a work system change, the better.

A manager must decide to be forceful at times or benevolent and understanding.

"Completely avoid delivering bad news, and you will get the reputation for being spineless. Cover yourself with mud too often, and you will make it impossible to hold a halo anywhere near your head. It's a tough balancing act."[45]

Performance appraisal is the process by which an organization establishes, measures and evaluates behavior. The performance appraisal is used to provide:
- Employee and managerial feedback
- Salary considerations
- Promotion
- Documentation

People want more without justification; therefore, create incentives so that their work contributions increase.

Sometimes people use humor or clowning when feeling overburdened with an inappropriate amount of responsibility.

Consider horizontal or lateral movement to develop multi-skilled workers.

A particular incident may reveal an individual's true character.

Pay plans that create worker conflict, not teamwork, are damaging.

---

[45] Peters, Tom. *Pursuit of Wow*. Reprinted in Success Magazine 11/94 issue. P. 58

Many people are not taught or do not understand problem solving skills; therefore, cause and effect relationships are poorly understood.

The existence of a difference in personal I.Q. is important to recognize, but not necessarily publicly acknowledge. The exact source of the difference be it genetic, environment, or economic is not important.

Overwork causes unhealthy and unproductive employees. Overworked employees can develop problems with morale, stress, irritability, anxiety, and resentment. These problems may also affect the employee's family life.

Identify developable skills in employees and implement training.

You make a choice to contribute or not.

Employees who are not promoted or given choice assignments may not like to admit some inadequacy, but prefer to blame someone outside themselves.

Jokes whose main purpose is to embarrass others are not acceptable in the workplace.

Link rewards to performance and responsibility.

It is not necessary to keep your employees happy by becoming a hostage to their demands.

An employee who constantly voices confrontational and disruptive opinions is in need of disciplinary action. The action is based on the severity of conduct and can range from a verbal warning to dismissal.

Recognition and reward systems fuel motivation; but if the system is not fair and unbiased, then the system becomes a problem.

All employees have the authority to make changes. It is the significance of the changes that an employee can introduce that is the variable.

As a manager you should find a way to help people make a contribution.

A good leader will search out the collective wisdom, accumulated judgments, perception, experience, intuition, and intelligence of people inside and outside the organization.

Maintaining an environment of performance expectations will assist motivation. An employee who is discharged for inappropriate actions may not be eligible for unemployment benefits.

A list of employee incentives that can be considered within a system of rewards is as follows:
- Money
- Recognition
- Time-off
- Part ownership
- Good assignments
- Advancement
- Freedom
- Personal growth
- Fun work
- Prizes

Make pay consistent with market forces.

Meeting deadlines is an important job performance criterion.

An employer's response to harassment is not measured by the victim's own sense of personal justice. Responses by the employer can include warning or relocation.

An employee who threatens others is a harasser and potentially subject to termination.

The immediate dismissal of an employee can be considered for the following reasons:
- Absence without reason
- Embezzlement
- Theft or unauthorized use of company property
- False or malicious statements about the company, customers, or co-workers
- Falsifying information on application, time sheets, expense forms

The ability to focus on the desired result is a special skill.

Consider changes in business system and employee rewards to create an empowered innovative workforce.

When considering a person for a position in your company, consider asking the following questions of his/her previous employer such as:
- Did you try to convince the candidate to stay?
- What type of work was the employee involved in?

Factors in employee selection are:
- Technical competence
- Book learning
- Experience
- Personality

You can't fire an employee because his coworkers don't like him unless the employee is a significant threat to employee morale or productivity.

Alcoholism is not a protected disability if it poses a direct threat to others in the workplace.

A medical exam may be necessary and can be ordered when an employee is having difficulty performing the job effectively.

Harassment behavior must be severe or pervasive enough to negatively affect the victim's working environment.

Change from a culture of entitlement that is based on seniority, to a culture of accountability that is based on results.

Spending money on employee training and learning programs are investments in your human assets.

Providing training and career advice to employees offer the following benefits:
- Presents new challenges
- Offers new perspectives on existing problems
- Encourages innovation
- Seminar attendance is a reward – a motivating experience

Job descriptions provide a base starting point. Unwritten job requirements often deal with intangibles such as:
- Being good listener
- Confidence to cope with rejection
- Love of detail or flexibility of action
- A type of behavior required such as talkative or silent
- Fit with the organizational culture

Stress in the workplace can be created by the following:
- Responsibility without authority
- Unpleasant working condition or unpleasant associations
- Inadequate recognition and reward
- Lack of clear job description
- Lack of job security

Highly desirable employees demonstrate the following characteristics:
- Initiative
- Networking
- Self-management
- Perspective
- Followership
- Leadership
- Teamwork
- Organizational skills

Requiring that an employee behave in a manner consistent with accepted social norms is a reasonable request.

Focus on improving behavior, not improving attitude. Requiring improved behavior from an employee will eventually result in an improved attitude.

Satisfaction is a function of the amount of influence you have over your work. Therefore, if possible, negotiate actions required rather than take orders.

Employee morale is based on relationships with other employees. People can poison themselves and others with hatred of work or others.

Management should provide enough organizational and bureaucratic structure to provide employee focus.

Every team requires a leader, and the leader gets to make the decision that he/she feels is best.

Create an organizational structure that is in line with current business conditions. Adjust the structure as conditions change.

Pay should equate to the value of a worker, and must by law be fair.

Chapter 7

The Culture of Innovation and Creativity

The performance of an effective leader requires a combination of the following:

A)   Strategic Focus

Developing strategy requires knowledge of the marketplace, technology, and company and information systems.

B)   Business Focus

The achievement of satisfactory business performance requires a broad range of knowledge in quality, problem solving, planning and job requirements.

C)   Workforce Focus

Developing your workforce involves coaching, facilitating, training, counseling, and motivating.

D)   Interpersonal focus

Involves communication, conflict resolution, negotiation, and the art of compromise.

E)   Personal Focus

Involves honesty, high energy, positive attitude, innovative and persistence.

The top 10 technology challenges as indicated in 1998 by Battelle Memorial Institute are as follows:

1. Convergence of technology at home

2. Human interfaces which will be pushed beyond user friendly to be pleasing to our senses

3. Personalized consumer products

4. Affordable home based health care

5. Nutritional health causing foods and packaging changes to increase vitamin content

6. Protecting the environment

7. Renewed transportation, water, sewage infrastructures

8. Mobile energy and efficient energy

9. Micro personal security

10. Global business competition

Too often people want to differ decisions and actions to the team. Often times this approach needs to recognize that decision making is by team, while decision taking is by individual.

There is a difference between creativity and innovation. Creativity is to dream ideas while innovation is to make the dream a reality.

All groups require a purpose, a reason to exist. Once understood, then all efforts should be directed toward your reason for existence.

The creative organization requires certain characteristics. The higher the degree that each characteristic is maintained, then the higher creativity potential of the organization.

- Involvement of people with challenging assignments.

- Freedom of information available to all members, accompanied low degree but necessary level of bureaucracy.

- Trust

- Provision of time to think

- An atmosphere where humor is accepted

- Low personal tension or conflict

- Idea conflict eventually culminating in idea refinement and support

- Risk taking

It is important to personally develop a mindset of searching and finding opportunity.

Strategic planning involves consideration of factors that may influence your operations. These factors include:

- Government trends

- Market trends

- Management trends

- Technology trends

- Client trends

- Product trends

If a product is designed to a customer's specification, then the product is not a standard item and cannot be sold to others without permission.

What do you like about work? The answer to this question may keep you from falling into a rut.

The sharing of information contributes to multi-skilled personnel. Therefore when you are preparing a report, database, or holding a meeting, then think in the broadest terms about who could possibly benefit and perhaps provide benefit.

If you empower people, then make sure that everyone has the same understanding of organizational goals. Empowerment is not abandonment.

Employees who lack the skill or interest to perform a job are mismatched. Their health and the health of the organization will suffer.

New ideas are fragile. Do not negatively evaluate too soon. Pick aspects of the idea that will work. Creative solutions depend on the discussion and refinement of multiple ideas.

Technology advancements are driven by the demands of the market. Therefore, technological developments must be applied to satisfy a customer's needs. These needs are generally not expressed in a direct manner, but usually must be ascertained by observation and analysis. Disagreements concerning the direction of technology can arise because the analysis involves interpretation of the observations and the opinions about the technology's capability to satisfy a need. A combination of facts with ideas usually leads to proper analysis.

The rapid pace of change creates instability that cannot be ignored or wished away. Seek to restore balance, if only temporary; you cannot ignore the dynamics of the worldwide market.

I noticed a want ad for the CIA, which stated that the CIA was looking for people having adventurous spirit, forceful personality, superior intellectual ability, toughness of mind, integrity, and professional discipline to produce results. I dare say that these same qualities are relevant to all organizations.

A technology strategy identifies ways in which the technology of the business will be used to achieve financial objectives.

Balance the importance of invention and production. Both require consideration and resources.

Foster teamwork by determining a goal or a rallying point for the good of the entire group.

Pursue continuous learning in response to continuous change. Some people are very protective of existing techniques and are not open to a different approach. Help them understand the personal benefit.

Conformity is the jailer of freedom and the enemy of growth. (John F. Kennedy)

An organization is a collection of individuals who jointly participate in moving to a new position.

Balance consistency and fairness. Fairness based on defined criteria and situational differences provides consistency.

Employees become irritated and resentful when some people receive privileges that appear to be unjustified. Employees understand justifiable privileges as benefits based on measurable results or contribution.

Share information with employees so that they feel important and develop a sense of belonging. Without proper information, people will not develop a shared purpose.

Share the benefits of organizational success with everyone.

Moving to a high productivity organization requires a cultural change.

Treat employees with honesty and respect, and expect honesty and respect in turn.

Automotive suppliers are involved in two relationships with customers. A maintenance relationship that involves satisfying current obligations and a partnering relationship that involves satisfying future needs.

A business turnaround strategy can be reduced to the following four actions:
- Reduce dividends
- Issue new debt
- Reward performance
- Eliminate poor products, poor performers, and any business redundancy

The organizational management model of the industrial revolution segments responsibility in the hierarchy as follows:
- Top management
  - Possess knowledge
  - Strategist
- Middle management
  - Controllers
- Frontline management
  - Implementers

The entrepreneurial management model changes the hierarchical responsibility to the following:
- Top management
  - Provide inspiration, value, challenge status quo
- Middle management
  - Interdepartment and customer coordination
- Frontline management
  - Key strategists and decision makers

The preferred approach by a manager should be as a facilitator, not a dictator.

Financial hostages in a company are created when bonuses or other rewards are a future event, dependent on continued results or employment. The employee will eventually seek this benefit (bonus) and later realize he/she is trapped because of his/her expectation and need. Once this happens, the employee can become resentful.

The system of rewards and punishment must be carefully structured to avoid favoritism or the appearance of favoritism.

Become a multi-product, multi-technology, and multi-market company.

Innovation requires continuous learning. The key is a change in your behavioral attitude that allows you to love learning.

Study other companies' products and services to determine if they are assuming innovative approaches. Consider if any approach that is discovered by this process can be applied to your organization.

Companies need to generate and explore of ideas because survival depends on having multiple explorations in progress.

Change yourself first then your associates then your organization.

It is easy to notice an organization with a culture that accepts and pursues change versus one that pursues the status quo and falls into oblivion.

Two aspects of a job are:
- Creativity functions
- Maintenance functions

Both functions are needed for sustainable growth.

Changes should be made before a disaster strikes.

Improvement activities may have their roots in the quality area. So, seek knowledge in the principles and practices of the quality tools.

Innovation and creativity are two items to look for in your suppliers.

Objective criteria should be used to determine the importance of an activity.

Begin each day anxious to learn and explore.

It is not possible to know if you are advancing unless you measure your steps.

Economic dislocation can be caused by changes in rules or regulations. Look at the economic crisis that have occurred, and you will see how the system created it.

Recognize that you do not always have the superior ideas. It is OK to advocate your own idea, but be open to other ideas by being willing to ask questions and actively listen.

To take advantage of an opportunity is similar to playing a game that requires offense or change. You cannot win the game by constantly playing defense.

Quality is secured thru standardized operations. But do not become so standardized and bureaucratic as to stifle creativity and innovation.

A company grows with new knowledge, so foster knowledge sharing.

A constant need to search outside the organization for fresh leaders is an indication of a cultural problem. The people within the organization are not being developed and nurtured.

Your company needs to operate with two simple ideas, which are:
- Being very responsive to customers
- Actively pursue new growth

Overhaul performance evaluations by emphasizing the development of new skills and behavior.

Unjustified favoritism seems to influence employee compensation. This creates low morale, resentment and conflict.

I believe that the future of innovation is in the convergence of technology. Individual breakthroughs are few and far between.

The economic health of nations is determined by productivity, growth, and their innovation rate in all areas of the society.

Constantly look for the opportunity to save your customers money without a sacrifice in quality.

A superior racehorse can win one race with any jockey, but the horse trainer is very critical to continued success.

Knowing your market demographics will assist in the determination of strategy. Figure 7 data indicates that older drivers are more likely to purchase an American car. The knowledge of this is important to establish product and technology strategies.

116

Figure 7 – Owner Loyalty[46]

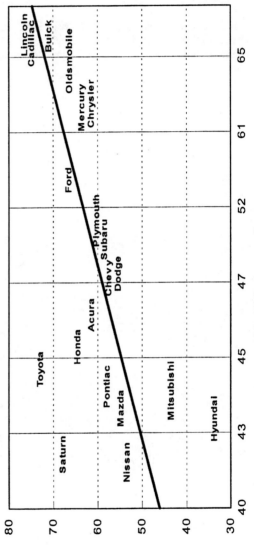

Vehicle Owner Loyalty

Conclusion: The older you are the more loyal to a brand of vehicle.

[46] Diem, William R. "Bond Stronger With Age" *Automotive News*, Volume #5544, Page S-6 and S-43

Hold to basic values, but adjust to change without causing irrevocable damage.

Develop personal initiative and individual accountability for yourself and your employees.

Eliminate your anxiety with action.

"Success is the ability to go from one failure to another with no loss of enthusiasm." (Winston Churchill)

Read, capture thoughts, and use a journal to capture ideas, meaningful sayings, and the guidance provided by others.

Create a supportive environment where people are free to be involved.

Unconventional processes can foster business advancement. For example, change the relationship between divisions by requiring a division to buy time or resources from a supporting division.

An organization is a spider web of formal and informal relationships. Pay attention to both types of relationships because a project can be informally derailed.

Subtly encourage self-motivation instead of forced motivation.

The term added value can mean adding financial value, teamwork value, or process value. Unfortunately, it is often interpreted in purely financial terms.

The book "The Human Equation" (Harvard Business School Press) offers seven practices that the successful companies share:

- Employment security

- Selective hiring of new personnel

- Self-managed teams and decentralization of decision making as the basic principles of organizational design

- Comparatively high compensation contingent on organizational performance

- Extensive training

- Reduced status distinctions and barriers including dress, language, office arrangements, and wage differences across all levels

- Extensive sharing of financial and performance information throughout the organization

Jeffrey Pfeffer, the author, concludes that high performance requires enriched work and good pay.[47]

Take the initiative, do not wait for instructions.

Pursue future technology investments to boost business results.

---

[47] Kinni, Theodore. "Why we Work" *Training Magazine.* August 1998. P. 34-39 Lakewood Publications

Chapter 8

Comparison of American and Japanese

Japanese companies are as political as any American company. Japanese executives may make a decision that allows them to avoid social embarrassment. A Japanese executive is usually not the expert, his staff is. The executive's job is a facilitator coach and relationship builder.

More than 50% of the population in many Asian countries will rank economic prosperity over political freedom. This ratio is much higher than in the United States.

A common opinion of politicians and business people in many nations is that the competitiveness of the country is damaged by emphasis on labor rights.

The competitiveness of any nation is influenced by the following factors:
- Political and social stability
- Government regulation
- Technology capability
- Openness of the legal system

Employee performance reviews in Japan are purposely obscure as a way of extracting maximum effort. Americans are, in general, more inclined to provide minimum effort under such circumstances because responsibilities and expectations have not been defined.

Americans tend toward conspicuous displays of wealth and individualism, while Japanese are more likely to focus on group harmony.

The Japanese conception of boss or leader is of a benevolent general. The American concept is of a knowledgeable leader.

Japanese have a tendency to rank the quality of items. This ranking involves most everything such as hotels, cars, companies, and people.

In a Kaisha (Japanese company) there is no universal rule, truth, or behavior to be applied in all circumstances. Context governs appropriate behavior (situational truth).

When an American is arguing a point with a Japanese, then it is useful to remember that logical arguments are only one view of the world. An uncharacteristic emotional response from the Japanese staff may occur if the Japanese staff member's view is not acknowledged.

International competition requires that the people within the organization possess international skill and knowledge combined with adequate nutrition, exercise, and an open mind.

If American employees working at an American subsidiary of a Japanese company, come to realize that the Japanese are there to bear the consequences of failures and that local employees are left out of the decision loop, then morale and enthusiasm will suffer. The blending of American and Japanese cultures at subsidiary operations is difficult because of language differences and individual versus group mindset.

It is preferable to refer to persons assigned overseas as an assigned employee.

In Japan, suppliers develop products by
- Contract on a program
- Mutual reliance (i.e. supplier risk on the project is compensated by another project if the original project is discontinued) – This honor system is not universal in the United States.

Some companies use their overseas business as an extension of domestic operations. This can cause serious human resource problems if cultural differences in the host country are not recognized and acknowledged.

It has been reported that the Japanese economy should be boosted by the following actions:
- Deregulation
- Emphasizing consumer demand
- Increasing imports

If central planning and control failed in communist countries, then it is reasonable to believe that it will fail in multi-national companies with far-flung operations.

Americans feel social and financial insecurity due to a lack of corporate loyalty for employees, anxiety about crime, and a culture based on consumption. Japanese have not been significantly exposed to these insecurity-producing factors.

Foreign companies can pursue two different policies when expanding overseas:
1. Maintain strong home country influence with superficial actions to local culture.
2. Integrate with a part of local culture wherein the stature of the subsidiary is independent.

The secret of success is to do the common duty uncommonly well.
(John D. Rockefeller, Jr.)

Business contracts in Asia are occasionally awarded by "negotiated tender" instead of "competitive bidding." This process is subject to a strong influence of the relationships between the parties.

The extent to which Human Resource management activities are successfully applied across cultures depends on the ability to balance other cultures values and practices in:
1. Importance of work
2. Work relationship to other life factors (personal)
3. Work relationship to the group
4. Power and status
5. Desirability of change

The legal system in the United States is dependent on traditional judges who are experts in courtroom proceedings. However, the specialized nature of a product case or a product defect investigation argues for a specialized judge. Arbitration is the corporate preference.

Over investment by Asian economies was seen as a prerequisite for sustaining economic growth. This approach is acceptable unless the economy slows down then the equipment building and plants introduced due to the over investment approach become burdensome and are seen as a structural problem.

The health, cognitive ability, and emotional development of any person anywhere in the world are influenced by low birth weight and poor socioeconomic class. Greater efforts to improve prenatal care should improve the competitiveness of any society.

Numerous articles have reported that the economic crisis in Asia that occurred during 1998 was influenced by government's treatment of banks. The banks were used as tools of state industrial development policies, oftentimes, making loans without securing adequate collateral. This policy did not adequately consider the capability of the market. Therefore, the future of Asian banks will consolidate on reduction of political and relationship based loans, and improvement in their loan risk analysis.

In Asia, business has developed based on personal relations, not binding contracts. It is also true that Western business is based on personal relationships, but a strong secondary basis of legally and financially binding agreement is in place.

There exist a web of social relationships that influences individual and organizational behavior. These relationships should be understood because of their effect on economic growth.

Welfare leaves behind a legacy of bitterness and mutual contempt. The United States and several European countries have a welfare system, which by comparison to Japan, Korea, and southeast Asia is very generous. The psychological cost of western style welfare without requirements to work is bitterness and contempt. The disadvantage of far- east welfare systems is untreated individuals left in poverty. A blend of systems is perhaps the best policy.

The effectiveness of the Japanese management system has been attributed to three items:
1. Unique industrial relations (permanent employee)
2. Unique financing (banks, not stockholders)
3. Unique industrial policy (government guidance)

Items 2 and 3 were used to provide a state guided central industrial policy. However, once Japan became a complex major economic powerhouse, then the capability of a central command and control structure to guide a complex society became problematic.

Personal and organizational change requires behavioral and cultural adjustments. A change in your beliefs is required to achieve a change in behavior. This change can only be accomplished by continuous learning and refinement. This approach is particularly important for employees of multi-nationals.

The mindset of a multinational organization should be equality of customers.

Employees should be chosen for flexibility and adaptability. This requirement becomes more important in subsidiaries of foreign companies wherein a mix of cultures exists. A person's willingness to learn, accept, and work in consideration of the boundaries of a different culture are an indicator of his/her contribution potential.

Migration patterns, not birth and death rates, are determinants of population shifts in the U.S.A. According to the statistical yearbook of the Immigration and Naturalization Service[48], the number of immigrant arrivals and the percentage of immigrants in the United States are increasing (See Figures 8 and 9).

---

[48] Cobb, Joe. "Immigration" Issues 96: The Candidates Briefing Book. The Heritage Foundation: Chapter 11

Figure 8 – Number of Immigrant Arrivals by Decade

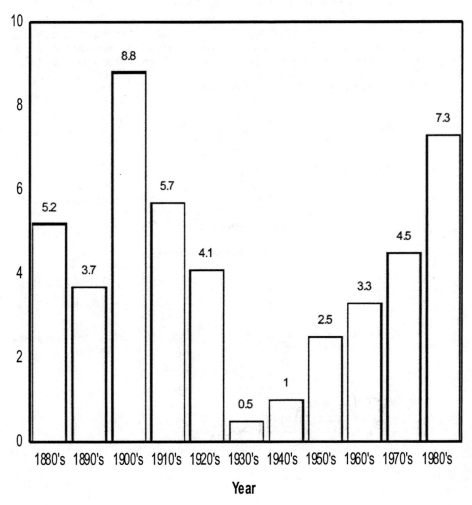

Source: Statistical Yearbook of the INS

The racial mix of recent immigrants to the United States is changing (see Figure 10) and the impact of immigration on certain states, such as California and New York, (see Figure 11) where immigrant destination is significant are still being developed. This demographic trend is a marketplace change, which will impact the types of business opportunities as well as social and legal considerations. This U.S. population and immigration situation contrasts with Japan, which has a projected average population increase of 0.22% versus 0.88% in the U.S. with low legal immigration, which in 1988 was 80,000[49]. Contrast this value to the U.S. value of 600,000 per year, which is 7.5 times greater than Japan. Additionally, the elderly population of Japan is growing at six times the rate in the U.S. Again, these dynamics reveal a marketplace of the future, which, without intervention, will be quite different than the U.S. market place.

As a nation's per capita income increases, then there is a customary change in spending patterns that are generalized as follows:

Level	Characteristics
1	Poor country status
2	Appliances are purchased to improve living standard
3	Cars and transportation become important
4	Bigger homes and domestic travel become commonplace
5	Overseas travel becomes common

Note: This scale is patterned after a similar pattern proposed by Mr. Gordon Wu, a Hong Kong billionaire.

Confucianism emphasizes education, order, and respect. This belief system was imported to Japan from Zen Buddhist monks.

Confucian ideals of hard work and loyalty have contributed to Japan's economic success. Other traits emphasized by Confucian ideals are:
- Responsibility
- Family

Confucian ideals are not widely accepted within the United States.

---

[49] Richman, Louis S. "The Coming World Labor Shortage" *Fortune*. April 9, 1990. P. 70

Figure 9 - Immigrants as Percentage of the U.S. Population

Immigrants as Percentage of the U.S. Population

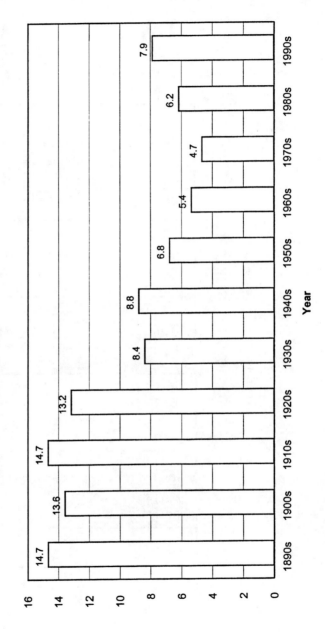

Source: Statistical Abstract of the United States

Figure 10 – Origins of Immigrants

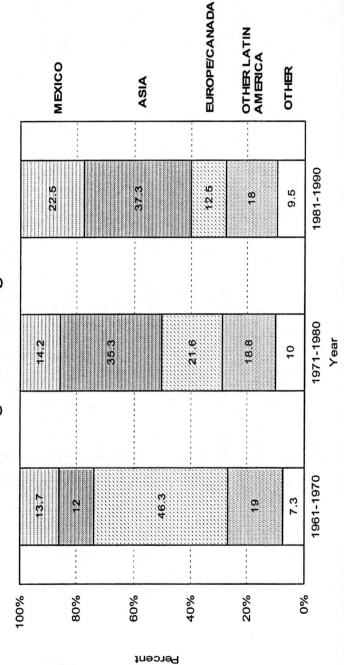

Origins of Immigrants

Figure 11 – Immigrant Destination by State

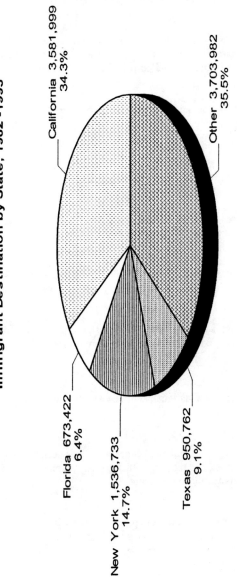

Immigrant Destination by State, 1982 -1993

California 3,581,999
34.3%

Other 3,703,982
35.5%

Florida 673,422
6.4%

New York 1,536,733
14.7%

Texas 950,762
9.1%

Source: Statistical Yearbook of the INS

Japan is poor in natural resources. Therefore, the most important resource is people and people should work together in harmony. This one factor explains the Japanese emphasis on being Japanese and the corresponding emphasis on an insular society.

A dinner in Japan is prepared by considering Buddhism, Zen, and Shinto principles. The color and composition give the meal balance and harmony (Buddhism), while subtle flavors is a Zen consideration and purity a Shinto consideration.

Purity and cleanliness are an important part of Japanese life due in large part to the influence of Shinto.

Knowledge of the culturally ingrained elements of an individual's personality will help you accept and positively interact with the person.

Zen Buddhism sees nature as symbolizing the cycles of life, just as the seasons change so our lives must change too. Zen stresses simplicity in all things.

Zen Buddhism stresses that attention should be given to even the simplest task, while the emphasis in the United States is more clearly based on task importance.

The Buddhist sense is that the things we cherish cannot last because everything changes and so this is what makes them beautiful. Nature is especially appreciated because each day is a change.

A patchwork system of situational solutions will develop in any society unless there is a guiding principle.

Customer partnering is an important concept that has been adopted differently in the east and west. In the west, it is recognized that partnering must be combined with skillful negotiation and contractual agreements.

Asians and South Americans want to pursue business with people that they trust and respect. The development of trust and respect takes time. North Americans believe time is scarce; therefore, there is reduced emphasis in trust and respect with an increased emphasis on legal agreements.

As your company expands to become international or transnational, then your home country customers should not dominate your vision. A more suitable balance is advised in recognition of your changing status.

Country and corporate activities are influenced by self-interest.

The United States emphasis is toward accepting people as our equal, not as our superior unless they are rich. Contrast this with other cultures wherein the superiority of another person may be a function of birth, education, and title.

Under the U.S. justice system, it is common that the attorneys for the defendant will make unproven allegations in order to place blame outside their client.

Japan is influenced by a common belief that the company is first, while the culture of the United States is influenced by a belief that the person is first.

The rise in the economic power of Germany and Japan during the second half of the 20th century was influenced by U.S. policies during the cold war. These policies favored containment of communism and did not favor the development of U.S. internal business and economic affairs.

Man should identify himself with the basic spirit of nature by contemplation. This is a Chinese religious belief, which is not identical to the Christian belief.

Prior to the Second World War, the state religion of Japan, Shinto, emphasized the divine ancestry of the emperor and by extension of the Japanese people.

The United States has a problem with a high quantity of litigation and unreasonable awards or settlements. I believe that this problem hinders the implementation of safety devices in cars. Circumstantial evidence is presented by Figure 12, which indicates that the United States has a disproportionate number of lawyers, when compared to Japan and Germany.

Figure 12 – Lawyers[50]

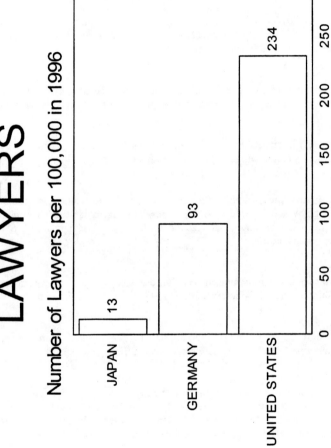

LAWYERS

Number of Lawyers per 100,000 in 1996

[50] Landers, Peter. "Great Expectations" *Far Eastern Economic Review*. Review Publishing, Woodside, N.Y.: November 12, 1998. P. 10-13

Freedom in the United States is reduced by people who are ready to explode into violence, particularly when agitated by hate speech, perceived rights, music, and movies. Some Asian societies such as Singapore and Korea have recognized the danger and have restricted access to these causal factors. Perhaps, we should restrict access as a response to our loss of freedom caused by our fear of predators.

Cross-cultural negotiations may require that you make statements or comments with self-confidence so that others will:
- Stop and think about what you are saying
- Be unnerved due to a suspicion that you know more than them

The culture in the United States seems to emphasize attributing blame. This emphasis is apparent in our legal system.

Those nations that do the best are the ones that reward hard work, responsibility, and thrift while accepting that mistakes are human.

The United States is a media saturated society. The increasing popularity of the internet indicates that other societies will become media saturated. Such a dominant influence can be exploited.

Many Americans believe that our value system is the standard by which others should be measured, just as our language is the standard.

American negotiators are generally thought to be more combative than Asian negotiators.

American should focus on the speaker's message rather than pronunciation, particularly when English is not the speaker's native language.

The belief that unrestrained individualism harms society and the economy is evidenced to some degree in all societies. The proper balance of individualism and community should always be a consideration.

Work to achieve better relations between cultures, particularly if you work in a multi-national company.

Patience and persistence are required in dealing with Japanese.

Japanese are not happy with someone who makes instant decisions. Being too decisive is seen as inconsiderate and not consistent with maintaining group harmony.

Japanese are generally quite proud of their company, but self-deprecating about their own involvement. Americans are generally more outspoken about their personal involvement.

A popular Japanese saying is Kyakusama Wa Osama, which means, " The customer is king."

The government of the United States should consider modifying programs that disrupt the family such as welfare without responsibility.

The United States must continually improve the quality of public schools, and foster a legal and social culture of personal responsibility.

If crime in America is a result of a lack of discipline by the family, schools, and society, then the solution must involve more discipline and less therapy for criminals.

Japan, France, and Sweden are producer-controlled environments, while the U.S. is a consumer driven environment. This difference has a major influence on marketplace dynamics.

Companies and countries may pursue programs that promote economic gain rather than maintaining social stability.

Schools should be a teacher of social conduct. Social conduct is a function of societal beliefs, which are grounded in religious concepts. Therefore, total separation of church and state is impossible.

Competition among companies is inevitable for economic development. A planned economy, which minimizes competition may allow rapid development, but does not always create an ideal society. Unfortunately, the final realization of this situation may surface unexpectedly.

Be aware of inflexible work rules, particularly from unions. Flexible workers operating in a flexible environment are necessary in the changing business environments that exist today.

Militant unions are created by militant management.

Listening without judgment, Zen Buddhists call this "bare attention". Listening sometimes requires impartial, open awareness.

Japanese national wealth owes a lot more to manufacturing excellence and export rather than skills at managing money.

The effect of world trade balances should be results oriented. Free trade as an ideological objective, which includes monetary trading, is not results oriented.

All countries use trade policy and public financial subsidies to achieve industrial policy. Disputes arise over the degree to which this is done.

There is a tendency for men to be transaction driven, while women to be relationship driven. Perhaps, this tendency also applies to west vs. east.

Japanese define integrity by behaving harmoniously and adjusting to the feeling of others. Americans define integrity as true to themselves.

The western style capitalist system is creative destruction that involves changes of the economic structure according to the marketplace.

Any society that intends to remain free and safe must place a premium on individual responsibility and personal accountability.

In business, you should be customer and region neutral. All business is important.

In Europe and Japan, there is limited pay for performance systems; so, organizations find other ways to motivate their people such as greater participation and communication.

It is generally accepted that Americans are less tolerant of class distinctions than other societies. This lack of tolerance, which has a historical basis and is a designed part of the American founding principles, is recognized by the lack of a monarchy or nobility class. Nobility classes receive favorable treatment and recognition as a function of birth without the need for demonstrating capability or responsibility.

Americans do not accept favoritism (high class assignment with favorable treatment) assigned simply by class ranking. Class distinctions which are individually earned by demonstrated capability, or hard work are accepted and provide encouragement for many people. Some examples of this earned nobility are Bill Gates of Microsoft, Henry Ford of Ford Motor Co. and Michael Jordan of the Chicago Bulls.

Americans are not tolerant of class distinction when the distinction is not based on understood action or demonstrated capability. The recent debate regarding the acceptability of affirmative action programs is influenced by this societal belief about demonstrated capability or action. In other words, Americans accept class distinction when justifiable and understood actions result in justifiable privileges. When the connection between action and privilege is lost but class distinction exists, then the following problems in the organization will become worse:

1. Lack of teamwork

2. Lack of common respect and trust

3. Lack of employee enthusiasm

4. Lack of employee involvement

5. Lack of employee loyalty (higher turnover)

6. Lack of coordinated office procedures

"If you know your enemy and know yourself, you need not fear the results of a hundred battles." Sun-Tzu. (The Art of War, 500 BC)

Christian ideas that may be applied to business are:
• Individuals should strive to improve the world by performing good work
• People should struggle for social justice
• Love everyone
• Forgive people for weakness

Chapter 9

Relationships and Alliances

A significant change in the composition of the workforce involves the increasing mix of part-time and full-time workers as shown in Figures 13 and 14. This trend creates new internal to external alliances to fulfill the employment needs.

A company must meet the demands of:
- Global integration
- Local differentiation
- High quality
- Low price
- Worldwide innovation

If the company is unable to meet these demands, then an alliance is required.

Companies must build truly strategic operations and global strategies within a local operations framework.

Recognize that business conditions may change during a project requiring adaptability. A company that was your competitor may become your partner or customer.

Wise advice when negotiating an alliance is sensible compromise, not senseless confrontation.

How successful a person or a company is able to mobilize resources is a key factor in the determination of the need for alliances.

Personal and business alliances depend on the chemistry of the individuals involved. Oil and water do not permit mixing.

It has been speculated that 75% of alliances fail because of the incompatibility of personalities or culture, while a smaller percent fail due to incompatibility of project priorities.

138

Figure 13 – Part Time Workforce[51]

PART TIME WORKFORCE

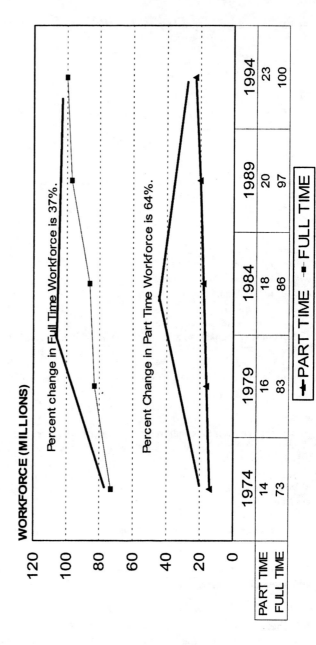

	1974	1979	1984	1989	1994
PART TIME	14	16	18	20	23
FULL TIME	73	83	86	97	100

WORKFORCE (MILLIONS)

Percent change in Full Time Workforce is 37%.

Percent Change in Part Time Workforce is 64%.

←PART TIME ■ FULL TIME

Figure 14 – Alternative Workers Benefits[52]

Alternative Workers Benefits

The following summary provides the percentage of companies that mentioned the reason why their company uses alternate workers i.e. to satisfy fluctuating production or to control cost.

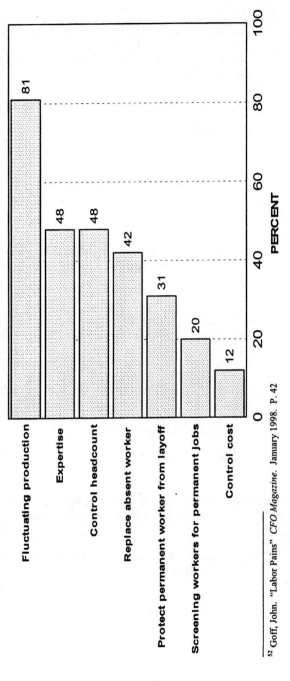

[52] Goff, John. "Labor Pains" *CFO Magazine.* January 1998. P. 42

When considering an alliance between two companies it is necessary to determine the phase that each company is operating in. A significant mismatch in the operational phase of the companies creates a more difficult alliance. Useful designations for operational phases are as follows:

1. Start up – risk takers and entrepreneurial activity

2. Revenue growth, expansion

3. Holding, risk averse

4. Declining

5. Renewal

The American automobile industry, which is confronted by high-labor cost, will continue to hollow out by outsourcing major modules. Eventually, major global suppliers will gain control.

Business alliance partners must discuss and agree on project priorities. The priority of a project is an indication of its importance. The agreement on importance means that the partners share a common understanding. The priorities can be assigned according to the following:

- High priority – This project significantly influences our survival or growth.

- Medium priority – This project is required to maintain position or slightly influence growth

- Low priority

Personal or corporate beliefs drive behavior. Therefore, unstated beliefs can be assumed by observing personal and organizational behavior.

Personal initiative and individual accountability are necessary features of a satisfying and productive alliance.

A person who can influence others, while also being open to someone else's ideas, is valuable.

Management must be willing to start up a team and develop them. This requires that the following activities occur:

- Recognize and workout personality conflicts

- Fight turf protection

- Provide goal unity

Economic power is about the aggregation of wealth and influence. Unequal economic power among supposedly equal partners creates a mismatch that can damage an alliance.

Projects or alliances require an orderly succession or transition. The smoothness of this operation can only be achieved by up-front planning.

If possible, do not dictate but seek agreement among members; however, if agreement cannot be achieved and project priority is such that actions are mandatory, then a dictatorial approach is required.

It is possible to limit a former employee's activity at a competing company. This can be legally done by emphasizing the potential for the misappropriation of the company's trade secrets such as price, business plans, product features, and specifications.

Operational support systems are necessary for creating and maintaining the business environment. The ISO standards provide a suitable reference.

Stay in touch with your customers and you will maintain a position in front.

Do not spend your time defending the past, better to focus on planning the future.

If your customers or partners present a dark and negative image about your alliance, then you should abandon your business or put substantial effort into relationship building.

Joining a team and playing for a team should be synonymous. If there is disconnect, then you must determine how a person becomes a full player.

It is a mistake to call a project or venture the president's plan, VP's plan, etc., because you share in the responsibility for success. Therefore, it is our plan.

You and everyone else in the organization are in a position to have a positive or negative impact. A manager's job is to encourage people towards the positive impact.

The following factors should be considered for any alliance or business relationship.

Objectives	Marketing	Marketplaces
Production	Strategy	Customer
Work	Product	People
Competition	Systems	Technology
Information	Management	Finance
Organization	Responsibility	Resources

Business can be initially based on informal relationship and personal trust. However, a more formal relationship is eventually required to clarify expectations.

The development of a positive relationship requires common priorities.

A successful blend of technical capabilities and people capabilities is required for smooth operations. People oriented tasks include:

- Building top management capability

- Building teamwork

- Improving quality awareness and the use of quality tools

- Providing training and new directions

Technical oriented tasks include:

- Designing product or process

- Identifying problems using engineering, accounting, or business skills

- Defining and implementing corrective action

- The pursuit of continuous improvement in operations

Some people or companies build business by knowing who, not knowing how. I believe that short-term success can be achieved by knowing who, but that knowing how is necessary for long-term survival.

Research conducted by the Wharton School found that a CEO's ability to command high pay depended less on skill and more on persuasion and manipulation of his board of directors.

Assess your team's strength so you can build on them. Identify weakness so you know where you need assistance.

Being an effective CEO requires leadership, not dictatorship. However, the two are not mutually exclusive.

The number of laws required by a society is inversely proportional to the morals of a society. This means that more laws are required, as a society becomes less moral. Interestingly, there is a German saying that states that the more laws, the less justice.

When considering an alliance involving partners from different countries, then consideration should be given to the influence of home country. A country analysis requires reflection upon the following characteristics:
- History
- Philosophy
- Culture
- Customs
- Pattern of behavior
- Nature of relationships

"It does not take much strength to do things, but it requires great strength to decide what to do." (Elbert Hubbard)

Decisions are difficult and not everyone will be happy. Therefore, a self-confident person is needed to undergo the rigors of implementing an unpopular decision.

The determination of business strategy involves consideration of economic, political, marketing, technological and competitive situations.

Horizontal linkage involves companies in the same business that jointly support R&D and coordinate design and manufacturing.

Generally, decisions that are made in the best interest of the company will be of benefit to the employees but not necessarily in the immediate future.

Personal conflict can be caused by not communicating, making assumptions, jumping to conclusions or sending a message in a way that is perceived as a threat or without justification.

The employees of an alliance have as much responsibility as managers do for creating a teamwork-oriented culture.

Acquisitions often fail because key people in the acquired company leave.

Europe is moving toward more open markets, which means greater market dynamics. The increase in the dynamics may create a need for more business alliances.

Global enlightenment and global commerce can be achieved by the internet.

When business use arbitrators to mediate a disagreement, then it is important to recognize the following limitations of the arbitrator:
- Not professionally licensed
- No particular legal knowledge required
- No discovery process is involved
- The company has the power to chose the individual

In voluntary arbitration agreement, the individual preserves the freedom to choose. The freedom to choose is reduced in binding arbitration, which is designed to provide a final resolution, not necessarily, a correct resolution.

Providing comfort and ego support is more important in relationships than skills such as persuasion.

People will self-select themselves out of a company culture that is not aligned with their wants and needs.

Business is run by economics, organizations are run by culture.

Companies entering a new region may focus excessively on sales workers. This emphasis is a demoralizer to your other workers because the emphasis creates a corresponding perception that workers in supporting roles are unimportant and, can therefore be, ignored or mistreated.

Disruptive group behavior adversely affects team morale. Disruptive behavior potentially involves any of the following, if done in extreme:
- Overly participative
- Under participative
- Aggressive or passive aggressive. Passive aggressive people remain quiet, but indicates contempt for others ideas.

Give competent people the tools and get out of their way. This approach is a silent affirmation of your confidence.

Program management is required because there is a need to plan, track, control, reallocate, report and decide. Program management involves these activities applied across functions.

Determining a company or a departmental culture may require an analysis of separate patterns of culture such as:

1. Power and influence

2. Individual roles

3. Rewards and accountability

4. Management style

When evaluating management style, consider how managers are valued and rewarded for their leadership skills. The following leadership skills are valuable:

*   Inspiring

*   Coaching

*   Planning

*   Organizing

*   Ability to exercise control

When considering acquisitions, it is advisable to perform financial due diligence as well as cultural due diligence.

The intended direction and results of a business or alliance are revealed by a consideration of the following factors:

- Key measures

- Key business drivers

- Organizational practices

- Leadership practices

- Work practices

- Technology use

- Physical environment

A leader needs to find ways to build enthusiasm and activity.

The best decision is dependent on your particular business and skill set.

A central office or government can be too far removed from the changing local environment and consequently incapable of directing activity.

The acquisition of technology is a major force behind the merging of industries and business.

It is necessary to gain and maintain the consent of those who work for you. This does not mean that they must like you, only that they respect you.

In a major transitional period authoritarianism leadership is required. The command responsibility that is required in a major battle must be accepted.

Business actions need to recognize that the judicial branch of the government is assuming more of a de facto legislative role, which can result in regulations without elected representation.

The ivory tower syndrome is a belief that only the opinions of intellectual or executive people are informed and to be considered. This may result in an inaccurate understanding of reality.

Informal dialogue to replace memos as the accepted mode of communication is desirable but impractical unless everyone is honest, trustworthy, and dependable.

A valuation of a company begins by considering assets, cash flow, management, market share, and price/earning ratio.

Sometimes less competent but highly ambitious people rise to a position of power and influence.

Supervisor and management personnel have a responsibility to conduct themselves as role models. It is a required that people in power set standards for others to follow.

Alliances and partnerships change the game overnight. Therefore, be prepared for possibilities and develop reactions.

The gathering, analysis, and reporting of information provides business intelligence. The information is useful in the following areas:

1. Support for strategic decision making

2. Providing early warning of opportunities and threats

3. Competitor assessment and tracking

4. Support for strategic planning and implementation

Business intelligence sources can include:

- Newspapers and magazines
- Press releases
- Research studies
- Litigation
- Human intelligence (information from employees, analysts, industry experts, contractors)

When in Rome, do as Romans because they are your customers and partners, but do not lose your own identity. Adapt, do not imitate.

A strategic alliance may be more suitable than a merger or acquisition. The decision depends on an analysis of business conditions, finances, skills, and culture.

Each company must be able to answer the question, "What do you regard as strategic to growth?"

Provide a common ground, common standard, common frame of reference when entering a negotiation.

Raise your productivity and wages will follow.

Many people build great businesses but along the way they abuse the people who helped make them great. They used people, not developed them. They told, not asked. In the process, they lost the loyalty and respect of the workers.

Happy business families of people or businesses can be thought of as satisfying individual needs of:
- Love
- Appreciation
- Communication
- Sharing
- Leadership

Democracy exists with a free and responsible press. Empowerment exists with a free and responsible workforce.

As Alfred Sloan said: "The professional manager is a servant. Rank does not confer privilege or give power, it imposes responsibility."

People learn as they work together toward the achievement of clear goals.

Trust is the foundation of any solid business and personal relationship.

A company culture in transition is bound to result in opportunity.

Companies or families with people in different locations need communication and cooperation mechanisms combined with clear responsibilities.

Doing business does not mean only selling; it means considerations of partners, suppliers, joint ventures, or alliances as well as human resources.

Changes in opinion can be made for economic reasons or altruistic reasons.

The responsibility of top management is to be proactive, instead of reactive to a customer problem. The fulfillment of this responsibility involves communicating, negotiating, counseling, and coaching.

Many managers do not like their new role as coach or advisor because it takes them out of the spotlight. Their egos cannot handle what is perceived as reduced status.

Management should identify problems and involve others to refine the definition of problem, then begin progress toward solutions.

To rationalize production means that a single plant should perhaps be sole source and totally responsible for a product. This approach allows focusing of resources.

Discussions and negotiations often involve give and take. This can result in emotional assaults on a negotiator. The negotiator requires a self-confident personality to cope with the assaults.

Intense competition and slim profit margins are a prelude to mergers and acquisitions.

The settlement of a confrontation requires engagement, not long-term isolation. Isolation leads to less confrontation but a more severe ultimate result.

Evaluate your environmental, quality, design, warranty concerns wholly apart from regulatory requirements and challenge yourself to develop solutions.

Alliances or other partnering requires a contract, and under contract law both sides must give up something of value in order to form a binding contract.

Social security benefits and senior discounts are based on assumption of needs vs. means tested benefits. Accepting assumptions rather than data can be problematical in business, as well as society.

Each member of the team must have the skills and ability to get the job done. Each must be trustworthy, accountable, responsible, and reliable.

When faced with a challenging situation, then go with the power at that time but also keep others from undermining your position.

Discussions with competitors are not of and by themselves illegal or collusion. Discussions may be organized as information exchange.

The fast paced flow of information results in an increased potential for miscommunication and misinterpretation.

All employees and management should have the same objective, particularly in partnerships.

A cornerstone of conservative economic policy is to require that the users of public services pay, not all taxpayers. This approach is consistent with a use tax.

Poor economic policies and political instability are problems in developing countries. This situation creates risk for any venture.

Competitiveness at the global level has made the pursuit of national industries obsolete. Unfortunately, this message has not been received and understood.

Valued suppliers to a company should be treated with honesty and long-term commitment.

The economy of a single nation is not independent; therefore, the goal should be to develop a competitive posture that recognizes a global business society.

A manager who locates and retains talented people is able to concentrate on broader aspects. Setting standards and norms of behavior and expectations is the job of a manager.

Maintain a degree of trust and openness with your partners and suppliers.

The markets have taken over the role of political rulers. The cross boundary capitalism must be more rigidly controlled.

Borders around countries are like borders around companies, erected to keep the outside out.

Chapter 10

You Need Continuous Improvement

A broad review of multiple topics is beneficial in dealing with change. This is so because a change in work process will often times involve technology, work relationships and skills required. The successful implementation of a changed process is influenced by individual motivation, attitude, adaptability, resourcefulness, enthusiasm and persistence. These capabilities and traits can only be refined by continuous learning. The following material is presented to identify and reinforce the need for continuous improvement.

An employee's success at a job within a corporation depends on:

- A positive attitude resulting in dedication to personal mastery

- Shared vision between employee and enterprise

- Knowledge of purpose

- Energy and enthusiasm to accomplish results

- A philosophy of continuous improvement in self, processes and products

Many people consider continuous learning to be expensive and time consuming and feel justified in not pursuing their education. They fail to realize that ignorance is no excuse and that lack of knowledge is self-limiting.

The maximum transfer of knowledge from outside business consultants occurs when an in-house person, who is motivated and enthusiastic, becomes interested and involved.

Reading and observing will provide you with a diversity of ideas and point of views. This information may then be applied as a particular situation warrants.

If you stretch your skills and knowledge beyond your current area of expertise, then you are taking control over what can happen for you, not to you.

Having a formal education does not mean that a person is adequately educated to handle matters involving his/her marriage, job, children, finances and health. Life requires knowledge in all of these areas and more, so always prepare.

A college education hopefully teaches one how to define and attack problems. Having the college degree is an indication of having the important qualities of self-motivation and persistence, but it is not an indication of having common sense.

Self- driven improvement is required because your career is your responsibility -- not the company's responsibility, not the government's responsibility.

A living thing requires nourishment. Nourish your mind, your spirit, and your body.

Deepening your professional knowledge in a particular subject area can be contrasted with mastering a wider variety of subject areas. An individual's aspirations will determine which path to choose for self-improvement.

Employee training classes are often accompanied by handout materials. The amount of handout material can be limited and focused to the exact content of the lecture, or the material distributed can be significant and diverse. The motive behind including a significant amount of handout material is to allow individual decision on the information that is useful, which is hopefully a sizable amount. The availability of this large volume of information does not mean that the information will be thoughtfully reviewed; therefore, improve the possibility by providing a one or two page summary of materials to improve the consideration.

Best performance is achieved by organizing jobs according to employee skills and interest.

An effective way of demonstrating knowledge in a field is by obtaining professional or organizational certification.

Recognize that academic education only provides a foundation, which skill certification and continued development activity build upon.

Diversity training is better when combined with genuine caring between individuals and an interest in friendship.

The ability to understand and solve business, personal, technical problems needs regular updating and expansion using continuous learning.

When an individual pursues professional certification, then he/she demonstrates:

- Motivation and time commitment
- Continued commitment to their the profession and their contribution
- Mastery of job knowledge through examination and recertification

Internal coaching is better than sending your employees out for training because the coaching is real time involving relevant experience.

Completing a training course and demonstrating competence in the topic are different. Hold employees accountable for justifying the time and money spent on training.

Everyone in the company requires continual training in some aspect of business or culture. An open and inquiring mind is all that is required to initiate a search for a subject.

Training allows employee empowerment. Empowering untrained people is chaos.

Education and training are interactive requiring an interesting presenter and an interested learner. The learner is more important than the presenter because the learner is ultimately responsible for his/her skill development.

There is security in employability; there is no security in a job or a company. Employability is a function of your continuous improvement.

The training of people begins by determining their current status. The type and amount of training required will vary according to the individual's placement in the following category:

- Not familiar with basic principles

- Skill development is required

- Advanced skill development is required

Your skills should be in constant renewal. The key is to be prepared because you too can be a victim of circumstances such as a layoff or a business closure that forces you into the job market.

The old employment policy of maintaining a job due to seniority is ended. You must be a contributor and as conditions change, your contributions must change.

Lifelong learning and specialized knowledge are the only way to remain competitive in the job market.

Select career and life priorities based on your own expert judgment, not someone else.

Benchmarking is a process involving the discovery of best practices at other companies. The potential benefits of benchmarking can only be realized when your business processes are understood and documented to allow comparison.

Applying different disciplines to problem solving requires broad knowledge and experience that can only be gained by continuous learning.

As General Douglas MacArthur said, " Security lies in our ability to produce." This comment is as true for individuals, as it is for nations. You cannot depend on job security to be provided by your age, race, disability, or longevity.

If leaders are made, not born, then the process of making a leader requires the acquisition of knowledge and skill.

A manager should develop process and leadership skill, while the engineer should develop technical expertise.

Employees have to understand the business, marketplace, and the changing technology if they are going to participate in it.

Worker responsibility and commitment is achieved by training and on-the-job application of the training received.

Training should focus on the development of skills that are necessary to the individual and to the organization.

The individual and the organization require a philosophy of constant improvement, not a philosophy of minimal compliance.

The arrival of the digital age means that scientists will have increasing clout in Washington, D.C. because of the combination of politics and technology.

Expanding everyone's understanding and contribution by sharing information and providing educational opportunities.

Socrates said, "The only good is knowledge and the only evil is ignorance."

A workforce focus on employee involvement and empowerment requires the development of teamwork skills.

An important item for businesses to understand is intellectual property, which consists of all patents, marketing intangibles (trademarks, names) copyrights, trade secrets, and know how that provide a competitive advantage to organizations and individuals.

The exact definition of quality, as provided by experts, varies. However, I believe that it is important to remember that quality involves the maintenance of people, as well as machines.

Everything moves toward disrepair and chaos unless energy is added. This law of thermodynamics applies to people, as well as machines.

As a person rises in the organization, he/she will discover that rank has privileges, but also demands.

Apply a structured and consistent questioning approach to define problems whether personal or professional.

A Change Leader needs to be a master of change. Without knowledge and continuous learning, you are a slave to change.

Management tends to prefer internally motivated workers because such workers are considered less problematic than workers whose motivation comes primarily from external sources.

Extend your activities beyond your normal limits. Exercising your mind will result in strength of character and improved flexibility.

Sometimes you can be concentrating too much on self-development activity, instead of performing a function of value to the company. Be on guard for overdoing development and underachieving work.

Companies may have a need for a new set of skills in the future. How are you preparing to satisfy this need? Don't go through life simply repeating your activities. Learn and apply yourself to approach new activities.

Transform yourself to take command of the situation.

Improve your basic skill levels to allow application in new and creative ways.

Awareness training is necessary to develop new attitudes or to change bias.

If you are involved in the independent pursuit of knowledge, then your actions may positively encourage others to follow.

The security of individuals and nations requires continuous development, not maintenance of the status quo.

Grow more and more comfortable in a job by continuous understanding, so that you can advance your career.

Learn manufacturing processes and flow so that you can accurately judge the merits of design and manufacturing proposals.

Theory based planning must be refined by information based planning. Seek out information; build your own knowledge library in order to apply theory.

<u>Success</u> written by Bessie Anderson Stanley in 1904.

"He has achieved success who has lived well, laughed often, and loved much; who has enjoyed the trust of pure women, the respect of intelligent men, and the love of little children; who has filled his niche and accomplished his task; who has left the world better than he found it, whether by an improved poppy, a perfect poem or a rescued soil; who has never lacked appreciation of earth's beauty or failed to express it; who has always looked for the best in others and given them the best he had; whose life was an inspiration; whose memory a benediction."

Develop your intuitive skills by reading and contemplation. Intuition becomes more important as you assume more responsibility.

Adapt and learn new technology skills so that you are prepared for the future.

"Confidence doesn't come out of nowhere. It is a result of something ...... hours and days and weeks and years of constant work and dedication." (Roger Staubach)

Divorce financial profits from the learning process and a company or economy stagnates.

Develop your intellectual capital just as you develop your other capital resources.

You can develop new skills through volunteerism and thus help yourself, your company and your community.

Do not think that if it is taught, then it will be used. Follow-up and on-going support is required to successfully apply training.

Education provides the bricks, but ongoing learning provides the mortar.

Education encourages people to take greater responsibility and challenges. Results are enhanced through the refinement of education by additional skill acquisition.

Sometimes you sell your skills to employers or customers, not your experience.

Improve your ability to anticipate change by constantly increasing your knowledge. You can be a change master by accepting responsibility for it.

Improve and change yourself first, before you try to improve others. Improvements of others cannot be achieved without their agreement.

Complete the foundation for positive organizational change by providing training, and then encouraging the application of the training.

Hold people accountable for their responsibility, otherwise, you will be very disappointed by the lack of results.

The job of a leader involves providing knowledgeable employees motivated toward a goal.

Intellectual knowledge should be accompanied by spiritual growth.

The will to succeed must be accompanied by the will to prepare.

Knowledge work involves judgment calls that are applied according to a particular situation. This situational dependence requires self-driven improvement.

Effective managers solve problems, while ineffective managers create and prolong problems.

Training is a critical part of continuous improvement. Preparation for the future requires knowledge of the past, the present, and the future possibilities.

The continuous increase of available knowledge emphasizes the need for lifelong learning.

The accumulation and application of knowledge makes continuous improvement possible.

Chapter 11

Change at an Automotive Supplier Company

The implementation of the QS-9000 business system required a fundamental change in the business operating philosophy at a Japanese-American Automotive Supplier location. All of the previously described experiences, knowledge, and intuition were required to successfully transition the supplier location from a relationship based operation typical of a small family run company to an organized continuous improving structure required by customers. This approach resulted in a meaningful system that was understood by employees and resulted in successful certification to the standard.

The supplier location began in 1979 as a sales office of less than 5 people with substantial control of business operation exercised in Japan. The supplier changed physical locations several times, added responsibilities to include engineering, distribution, quality and strategic planning and changed the number of employees from less than 5 to approximately 100 in a 20 year time span. The dramatic change in organizational responsibilities and size were not accompanied by a dramatic change in the business operating system. The original operating system was adjusted to suit new circumstances on an ad-hoc basis, but a step back approach involving a more holistic consideration of operations was not performed in earnest until the mandatory QS-9000 certification requirement was implemented by the American Automobile Manufacturers.

The process of instituting such a significant change was assigned a Change

Leader and began in mid-1994. Certification was achieved in late 1996, an effort of over

2 years.

The chronology of significant events as recorded by the Change Leader follow:

Date	Activity
1994	Steering committee comprised of 8 members. The purpose of the committee was *Study QS-9000 standard to determine suitability *Review formats *Setup subcommittees for further work
1994, 1995	Lead Auditor training for several managers.
1995	Implement QS-9000 training for all managers, including an audit of new and existing business system material.
1995, 1996	- 3 audits conducted by outside consultants - Employee training
1996	- Continued employee meetings and training by VP and outside consultants. - Certification achieved

A review of the chronology of events indicates that the implementation of the

organizational changes and required support of the change initiative by using outside

consultants. This observation would seem to negate the central theme that effective

preparation of a Change Leader by training, experience, and thoughtful reflection in

multi-disciplinary areas including different cultures will lead to successful

transformation. However, the exact opposite is true; which is that Change Leader preparation is a necessary prerequisite for success with the caveat that a sufficient number of additional Change Leaders are required in an organization so that the momentum is maintained. The additional change leaders were provided by the consultant organization, who were sufficiently knowledgeable, dedicated and prepared to provide the necessary momentum.

Specific instructions were provided to Engineering and Sales departments to assist in the preparation of documents. The documents were to be organized within a loose framework of individual department manuals. This approach was considered to be consistent with the supplier's operating system history. However, the results of this approach proved to be inadequate due to a lack of centralized authority, coordination and control. Therefore, the decentralized, empowered approach based on the historical structure was abandoned in favor of a centralized control approach.

The centralized approach required the addition of temporary staff (consultants) that provided the following knowledge and skills.

1.   QS-9000 standard, TQM and practical industry experience
2.   Business Operating Systems
3.   Coordination and teamwork experience
4.   Experience with the management of change.

The consultants and I initiated work on a centralized operating system using the following approach:

1.   Identifying each departments activity and interactions

2.   Identifying and implementing a common document format

3.   Expanding formal and informal training material.

Sales Department Activity

1. **Forcing functions:**

   A. QS-9000 is a basic business organization system and philosophy. The Big 3 requires this system and its intent.
   B. A business system is required due to our growth in personnel and sales that requires structured chaos. This approach will result in the following:
      - Improvement in workload efficiency and effectiveness
      - Permit ongoing analysis and improvement of "we have always done it this way."
      - Allow for transfer and training of employees
   C. Document what you do and do what you document according to sound business practice while maintaining flexibility and innovation. This is the QS-9000 basic need.

2. **Sales applicable sections of the QS-9000 standard that are reflected in the "Business Operating System" manual:**

A.	2.0	Mission	4.3.	Contract Review
B.	4.1	Office Responsibility	4.4.	Design Change
C.	4.1	Sales/Marketing Personnel	4.5.	Product
D.	4.1	Metrics	4.14	Corrective Action
E.	4.2	Procedure	4.16	Records
F.	4.2.	Quality Planning	4.18	Training

3. **Sales procedures requiring Sales Department development**

   A. Sales Activity (Function, Responsibility, Reference)
   B. Customer QS-9000 Submission
   C. Program Issues Transfer Flowchart
   D. Launch Review Procedure (monthly meeting?)
   E. Customer Reports Procedure
   F. New Business Release Procedure
   G. P/N Release Notification
   H. Sales Metrics Requirements
      - Price/Profitability
      - Market Strategy Report
      - Market Share
      - Competitive Reporting
   I. Product Literature Preparation
   J. Customer Shipment/Scheduling Procedure
   K. Show Procedure and Approvals

Engineering Department Activity

1. **Forcing functions:**
   A. QS-9000 is a basic business organization system and philosophy. The Big 3 requires this system and its intent.
   B. A business system is required due to our growth in personnel and sales that requires "structured chaos". This approach will result in the following:
      - Improvement in workload efficiency and effectiveness
      - Permit ongoing analysis and improvement of "we have always done it this way".
      - Allow for transfer and training of employees
   C. Document what you do and do what you document according to sound business practice while maintaining flexibility and innovation. This is the QS-9000 basic need.

2. **Engineering applicable sections of the QS-9000 standard that are reflected in the "Business Operating System" manual.**

A.	2.0	Mission	4.2	Quality Policy
B.	3.0	Quality Policy	4.4	Design Control
C.	4.1	Responsibility	4.5	Product
D.	4.1	Engineering	4.8	Inspection & Test
E.	4.1	Metrics	4.9	Test Equipment
F.	4.2	Procedure	4.14	Corrective Action
G.	4.2	Document Approval	4.16	Records
H.	4.2	Reference Documents	4.18	Training

3. **Engineering procedures requiring Engineering Department development**
   A. Engineering Activity (Function, Responsibility, Reference)
   B. Customer Design Review Procedure
   C. Lab Test Procedures
   D. Launch Review Procedure (Monthly Mtg.?)
   E. Customer Reports Procedure (Problem Solving/Technical Reports)
   F. New Business Timing & Reporting Procedure
   G. Production Part Approval Procedure
   H. Design Inputs/Outputs Standard
   I. Competitive Analysis
   J. CAD Drawing Preparation and Transfer
   K. Design Verification
   L. Design Change Transfer & Identification
   M. Customer Installation Standard
   N. Test Part Handling, Storage, Packaging
   O. Records Control
   P. Engineering Metrics (ex. # Product Changes, Reliability vs. Competition, Customer Satisfaction, Program Timing Status, Product Features vs. Competition, Major/Minor Issues (FMEA, Assembly, Test, Manufacturing))

Document Format

Procedure Document Format

- **Title**
- **Purpose**
- **Scope**
- **Responsibility**
- **Procedure/Flowchart**
- **Definition**
- **Associated Documents**
- **Governing Policy**

Instruction Document Format

- **Title**
- **Purpose**
- **Part Description (Name/Number/Defined)**
- **Customer Part Description**
- **Responsibility**
- **Definitions**
- **Instructions/Flowchart**
- **Associated Documents**
- **Governing Policy**

Additionally, specific advice was provided to each departmental manager using bulletins such as the following:

Business Transformation Advice

A. PLAN

1. Understand the QS-9000 section for which you are responsible for and any associated relevant sections.
2. Review all current documents and outside documents which may be related to your sections to determine if such procedures/work instructions are acceptable to QS-9000 and to you.
3. Review the material distributed which listed the procedures required. Note that this list is adjustable by you if necessary, for example, by combining documents.

B. DO

1. Combine previous department documents and any new information. Rewrite a draft of any document and provide to associates for review and discussion. Review material with the Change Leader.
2. Develop your department list for work instructions, forms, and records required. Discuss with outside consultants and the Change Leader.
3. Hold meetings with your staff weekly to discuss each element of QS-9000 and to understand the latest documents issued. Use the Master Document List to assist meeting reviews and to develop office understanding of the system.

C. CHECK

1. Submit all material for review; document formatting, numbering and typing.
2. Review and approve returned typed documents for your department.
3. Search for review and relevant documents, using the Master Document List, which influence your department and which may result in an adjustment to your documents.

D. ACT

1. Make sure that your procedures/work instructions/forms/record keeping are in effect in your area and are being followed.
2. Create new documents, as necessary, to meet the intent of QS-9000.
3. Make sure that your department's important records are properly organized and easily available. Provide this information (record type, location, file sequence) to the document control clerk.

Note: The Plan, Do, Check, Act cycle (Shew Hart) is a specific tool that is applied here as a management tool to aid the organizational transformation.

Chapter 12

What was Learned and What can be Learned

The preparation of this book has taken over six years; the transformation of the organization was achieved in approximately two years, while my personal preparation, as a Change Leader, will continue for my lifetime. I began this book by discussing life and career changes and the resulting confusion and uncertainty that I felt. I have ended with a case history review of an automotive supplier that was required to implement a significant business operating system change. In retrospect, one important point that I learned from the case history was that an individual may not always make a right decision for a specific event, but must learn to create a combination of decisions that are right. The task of the Change Leader, for which I was chosen, would have been more difficult without the benefits that my wife, my children, my parents, my brother and sisters, my ongoing training, and my jobs have contributed. In particular, my wife Marsha taught me, through her coping with health issues, the value of a positive attitude. In fact, her positive attitude has been a beneficial influence on our children, parents and others as well. Learning to positively look forward instead of negatively looking back is the gift my wife gave me. I believe that the best advice I can give to anyone attempting to implement change is to develop your positive attitude and to constantly prepare yourself, because you cannot be sure what will happen.

Each individual needs to bring multiple experiences and broad knowledge to bear on problems and incorporate the application of varied disciplines to problem solving such as legal, technical, psychological, cultural, and social. Each individual can be sure that they can survive when change is ringing because they have developed the reserve energy from continuous acquisition of knowledge, skills, spiritual and emotional support.

The result of the case study combined with the conclusion herein, was to develop a set of Skill Guidelines for all employees. It is understood that the business transformation that was achieved can only be sustained through the continuous improvement of leaders and employees according to the Skill Guidelines map. As change rings, we will all be ready to answer the bell.

Skill Guidelines

(Determine the current capability of each employee and his/her need for additional training to be considered for other positions)

Required skills	Subject or Topic (Examples)	Applicable Job	Potential Training Sources	Continuous Learning Need
Communication	Writing Reading Listening Speaking	Secretarial especially. All, however jobs involving greater customer or supplier interaction require a high level of skill (beyond high school). These jobs are typically found in Engineering, Quality, Sales and Warranty.	*Local Community Colleges * At-home Study Programs *Adult Continuing Education * University Degree Programs * Seminars	YES Skill updates may be required within each 5 year period, particularly, if job responsibilities change to a more demanding area.
Teamwork	Interpersonal Relations Conflict Resolutions Stress Diversity Cultural	All. Jobs of a supervisory or managerial level will require high skill.	* Adult Continuing Education * University Degree Programs *Seminars	YES Skill updates may be required within each 5 year period, particularly, if job responsibilities change to a more demanding area.

Skill Guidelines continued …..

Required skills	Subject or Topic (Examples)	Applicable Job	Potential Training Sources	Continuous Learning Need
Personal Attributes	Leadership Professionalism Coaching Change Agent	Managerial	* Local Community Colleges * At-home Study Programs * Adult Continuing Education * University Degree Programs *Seminars	YES Maintaining knowledge in managerial areas is critical to organizational success.
Manufacturing Principles	Lean or Agile Manufacturing Theory of Constraints Component Manufacturing	Engineering Quality Sales	* Local Community Colleges * University Degree Programs * Seminars	YES Updates are required. Most likely some classroom activity once per two years.
Reliability	Probability Probability Distributions Forecasting FMEA APQP Design Design Standards QS-9000	Engineering Quality Sales Managers (All for QS-9000)	* Local Community Colleges * At-home Study Programs * Adult Continuing Education *University Degree Programs *Seminars	Pass CRE exam or extended learning every 2 years.

Skill Guidelines continued .....

Required skills	Subject or Topic (Examples)	Applicable Job	Potential Training Sources	Continuous Learning Need
Quality	Flowcharting Problem Solving Control Charting & SPC 7 Quality Tools Customer Requirements QS-9000 Auditing Statistics	Engineering Quality Sales Managers (All for QS-9000)	* Local Community Colleges * At-home Study Programs * Adult Continuing Education *University Degree Programs *Seminars	Pass CQE exam and CQA exam or extended learning every 2 years.
Project Management	Project Management Reporting	Sales	* Local Community Colleges * At-home Study Programs * Adult Continuing Education *University Degree Programs *Seminars	No
Business	Budgeting and Accounting Product Innovation Multinational Work Delegation Culture and Language Leadership Total Quality Management	Sales Engineering Management	* Local Community Colleges * At-home Study Programs * Adult Continuing Education *University Degree Programs *Seminars	Yes. 1 course every year.

Skill Guidelines continued ......

Required skills	Subject or Topic (Examples)	Applicable Job	Potential Training Sources	Continuous Learning Need
Ergonomics	Workplace Safety	Warehouse Inspection Repair Engineering	* Local Community Colleges * At-home Study Programs *Adult Continuing Education *University Degree Programs *Seminars	Update as needed.
Finance	Accounting Budgeting	Accounting	* Local Community Colleges * At-home Study Programs *Adult Continuing Education *University Degree Programs *Seminars	Update as needed.

Skill Guidelines continued ....

Required skills	Subject or Topic (Examples)	Applicable Job	Potential Training Sources	Continuous Learning Need
Vehicle Systems	Emissions Safety Charging Audio Navigation	Sales Engineering Management	* Local Community Colleges * At-home Study Programs *Adult Continuing Education *University Degree Programs *Seminars	Yes. 1 course every 2-3 years.
Technology	Navigation Obstacle Detection Wireless	Sales Engineering Management	* Local Community Colleges * At-home Study Programs *Adult Continuing Education *University Degree Programs *Seminars	Yes. 1 course every 2-3 years
Computer and Office Skill	Microsoft Graphing BPCS Forecasting Flowcharting Information	All	* Local Community Colleges * At-home Study Programs *Adult Continuing Education *University Degree Programs *Seminars	Certification programs are available such as Microsoft Certification.

Skill Guidelines continued ……..

Required skills	Subject or Topic (Examples)	Applicable Job	Potential Training Sources	Continuous Learning Need
Human Resources	Performance Review Discipline ADA Harassment	HR persons and all other employees to receive briefing.	* Local Community Colleges * At-home Study Programs * Adult Continuing Education *University Degree Programs *Seminars	Update as needed.
General	Cost of Quality Design of Experiments Correlation &Regression Metrology CAD	Anyone	* Local Community Colleges * At-home Study Programs * Adult Continuing Education *University Degree Programs *Seminars	Update as need.

Works Cited

1. Albert, Kenneth J. Ed.. *Handbook of Business Problem Solving*. New York: McGraw-Hill, 1980.

2. Benson, Tracy E. "TQM A Child Takes A First Few Faltering Steps." *Industry Week*. April 5, 1993: *242, 7,* 16-18.

3. Block, Steven R. "Put Team Spirit to Work." *Chemical Engineering*. February 1993: 119-122.

4. Bittel, Lester R., and Ramsey, Jackson E. *Handbook for Professional Managers*. New York: McGraw-Hill, 1985.

5. Burgelman, Robert A., and Maidique, Modesto A.. *Strategic Management of Technology and Innovation*. Homewood: Irwin, 1988.

6. Braude, Jacob M., *Complete Speaker's and Toastmaster's Library*. Paramus, N.J.: Prentice Hall, 1992.

7. Byham, William C., and Dixon, George. *Shogun Management*. New York: Harper Collins, 1993.

8. Chowdhury, Subir, and Zimmer, Ken. *QS-9000 Process*. Chicago, Irwin, 1996.

9. Cound, D. "Quality First." *Quality Progress*. March 1986: *19,3* 19-21.

10. Covey, Stephen R.. *The 7 Habits of Highly Effective People*. New York: Simon & Shuster, 1989.

11. Cribbin, James. *Leadership Skills for Executive*. U.S.A.: American Management Association, 1972.

12. Deep, Sam, and Sussman, Lyle. *Smart Moves For People In Charge*. Reading, MA.: Addison-Wesley, 1995.

13. Deep, Sam, and Sussman, Lyle. *Yes You Can*. Reading, MA.: Addison-Wesley, 1996.

14. Demente, Boye. *Japanese Etiquette & Ethics In Business*. Lincolnwood, Ill.: NTC, 1991.

15. Diem, William R. "Bond Stronger With Age." *Automotive News*: March 28, 1994, S6-S43.

16. Drucker, Peter. *Management.* New York: Harper and Row, 1973.

17. Emery, Charles R.; Summers, Timothy P.; Surak, John G., *The role of organizational climate in the implementation of Total Quality Management.* Volume 8, Journal of Managerial Issues, 12-22-1996, pp 484(13)

18. Gitlow, Howard S. "Understanding Total Quality Creation: The Japanese School of Thought." *Quality Engineering.* 1995: 523-542.

19. Goff, John. "Labor Pains." *CFO:* January 1998.

20. George, Stephen. *The Baldrige Quality System.* New York: John Wiley & Sons, 1997.

21. Goleman, Daniel. *Emotional Intelligence.* New York: Bantam, 1997.

22. Goode, Erica E., and Wagner, Betsy. "Does Psychotherapy Work." *U.S. News & World Report.* May 24, 1993: 57-65.

23. Harvey, Eric, and Ventura, Steve. *Walk Awhile In My Shoes.* Dallas: Performance.

24. Henderson, Lynne, and Zimbardo, Phillip. "Shyness." *Encyclopedia of Mental Health.* San Diego: Academic Press.

25. Hoecklin, Lisa. *Managing Cultural Differences – Strategies for Competitive Advantage.* Wokingham, England: Addison-Wesley, 1995.

26. Hope, Jeremy, and Hope, Tony. *Competing In The Third Wave.* Boston: Harvard Business School Press, 1997.

27. Imai, Masaaki. *Kaizen.* New York: McGraw-Hill, 1986.

28. Juran, J. M. Ed., Jurans Quality Control Handbook. New York: McGraw-Hill, 1998. Fourth Edition.

29. Juran, S. "Catching Up: How Is The West Doing?" *Quality Progress.* November 1985: *18-11*, 18-22.

30. Karen, Robert. "Shame." *The Atlantic Monthly.* February 1992: 40-70.

31. Kelley, Robert E. *How To Be A Star At Work.* New York: Times Books, 1998.

32. Kinni, Theodore. "Why We Work" *Training.* August 1998: P. 34-39.

33. Lamprecht, James L. *ISO 9000 Preparing for Registration*. Milwaukee: ASQC Quality Press, 1992.

34. Landers,Peter. "Great Expectations." *Far Eastern Economic Review*. November 12, 1998. P. 10-13

35. Lawrence, Paul R.. "How To Deal With Resistance To Change." *Harvard Business Review*. May-June 1954: 36-44.

36. Leeds, Dorothy. *Smart Questions*. New York: McGraw-Hill, 1987

37. Lieber, Ronald B.. "How Safe Is Your Job." *Fortune*. April 1, 1996: 72-80.

38. Lienert, Paul. "Family Income Needed To Buy Car Is Rising Again." *Detroit News*, August 21, 1996.

39. Lighti, Larry. "The List Pink Slip Blues." *Business Week*. May 19, 1997: 6

40. Odiorne, George S. *MBO II A System of Managerial Leadership for the 80s*. Belmont: Fearon Pitman, 1979.

41. Ohmae, Kenichi. *The Mind of the Stragegist*. New York: Penguin, 1983.

42. Parisi, Anthony J. Ed.. "The Quality Imperative." *Business Week*. October 25, 1991.

43. Peters, T., and Waterman, R, In *Search of Excellence*. New York: Warner, 1984.

44. Peters, Tom. *Thriving On Chaos*. New York: Harper & Rowe, 1987.

45. Richman, Louis S.. "The Coming World Labor Shortage". *Fortune*. April 9, 1990: P. 70.

46. Peters, Tom, *Pursuit of Wow*. New York: Vintage, 1994.

47. Porter, Michael E.. *Competitive Strategy*. New York: The Free Press, 1980.

48. Pritchett, Price, and Pound, Ron. *A Survival Guide to the Stress of Organizational Change*. Dallas: Pritchett & Associates, 1995.

49. Raudsepp, Eugene. "Coping With Anger." *Machine Design*. May 9, 1994: 79-84.

50. Sayle, Allan J.. *Management Audits*. Great Britain: AJSL, 1988.

51. Schmidt, Warren H. and Finnigan, Jerome P. TQManager. San Francisco: Jossey-Bass, 1993.

52. Segil, Larraine. "Alliances Depend On Chemistry." *Electronic Business Today.* June 1997: 16.

53. Senge, Peter M.. *The Fifth Discipline.* New York: Currency Doubleday, 1990.

54. Sheridan, John H.. "Lessons From The Best." *Industry Week.* February 15, 1993: 54-63.

55. Sheridan, John H.. "Culture Change Lessons." *Industry Week.* February 17, 1997: 20-34.

56. Sorge, Marjorie. "UAW Walks A Tightrope Between Old And New Jobs." *Wards Auto World.* June 1993: P. 38.

57. Teresko, John. "Be Customer Driven, Not Function Driven." *Industry Week.* August 2, 1993: *242, 15* 20-25.

58. Unknown. "Families Without Kids", The Economist, November 27, 1999. P. 27.

59. Unknown. *QS-9000 Automotive Engineering.* Warrendale, PA: SAE

60. Vass, Dianna, J. and Kincade, Doris H. *Relationship of TQM Implementation and Employee Opinion Survey: A Study of Three Manufactures.* Quality Management Journal: Volume 6, Issue 1, 1999.

61. Weinig, S. "Productivity Gains Still People Dependent." *Industry Week.* June 23, 1986: 14.

62. Yoshimura, Noboru, and Anderson, Philip. *Inside the Kaisha.* Boston: Harvard Press, 1997.

ISBN 155212352-9